UNIVERSITY CASEBOOK SERIES

INTRODUCTION TO ADVOCACY

RESEARCH, WRITING, AND ARGUMENT

EIGHTH EDITION

Edited by
ALISHA CROVETTO
JOSHUA SEKOSKI
Board of Student Advisers, Harvard Law School

FOUNDATION PRESS

This publication was created to provide you with accurate and authoritative information concerning the subject matter covered; however, this publication was not necessarily prepared by persons licensed to practice law in a particular jurisdiction. The publisher is not engaged in rendering legal or other professional advice and this publication is not a substitute for the advice of an attorney. If you require legal or other expert advice, you should seek the services of a competent attorney or other professional.

Nothing contained herein is intended or written to be used for the purpose of 1) avoiding penalties imposed under the federal Internal Revenue Code, or 2) promoting, marketing or recommending to another party any transaction or matter addressed herein.

University Casebook Series is a trademark registered in the U.S. Patent and Trademark Office.

COPYRIGHT © 1970, 1976, 1981, 1985, 1991, 1996, 2002 FOUNDATION PRESS
© 2013 by LEG, Inc. d/b/a West Academic Publishing
610 Opperman Drive
St. Paul, MN 55123
1-800-313-9378

Printed in the United States of America

ISBN: 978–1–60930–308–2

Mat #41394660

PREFACE

Most first-year law students are required to take a course in legal research, writing, and oral advocacy, or to participate in a moot court program. Of the many interesting courses you will have during your years in law school, your lawyering course will be among the most useful. Learning to be an effective advocate takes time and practice, but law schools recognize that an introduction to the basic skills is an important component of every lawyer's education. An introductory lawyering course may be the only opportunity you have to translate your classroom learning into practical work before you take your first legal job.

This book focuses exclusively on the litigation model of dispute resolution, because that is the model emphasized in many first-year courses. However, the emphasis on litigation belies its importance in American legal practice. Much of what is thought of as litigation settles before either party ever appears in court; lawyers spend a substantial amount of time advising clients rather than prosecuting or defending cases; and negotiation and mediation are fast becoming preferred means of resolving disputes. Nonetheless, every lawyer is well-served by a solid foundation in written and oral advocacy skills.

To help you sort through the legal problems presented in your lawyering course, this book analyzes the various stages of work you will do to reach resolutions. It begins with the moment when you first learn the factual context of a potential case and ends with oral argument, after you have researched and analyzed possible claims and defenses, as well as briefed the most persuasive arguments for your side. Examples are drawn from *Bell-Wesley v. O'Toole*, a hypothetical wrongful pregnancy action brought by the parents of an unplanned child against the doctor who negligently performed the father's vasectomy. The full record and appellate briefs for both sides appear in Appendices C, D, and E.

Each chapter is designed to be self-contained. If your task were to prepare a legal research memorandum on the strengths of possible claims, you could read this book through Chapter 4, "Writing a Legal Research Memorandum." Furthermore, many issues are briefed but never argued orally because of judicial time constraints. Thus, on a motion for summary judgment, you might have to provide a memorandum of points and authorities opposing the motion (a "brief") for the court, but would not necessarily need to prepare for oral argument. In that case, you could profitably review the chapters on legal research, rule synthesis, and writing a brief without concerning yourself with other topics. You should view this book as a resource to accompany you as you become familiar with legal advocacy; adapt it to fit your individual style and needs.

One final and very important point is that you will need to make strategic and stylistic choices throughout the process of handling a given legal problem. The art of advocacy is necessarily a product of your own tastes and personality. There is no "right" way to research an issue, write a memorandum, or draft a brief. This book offers you alternatives wherever possible; you should choose among them at will. Any attempt at prescription would be foolhardy; take advantage of the many colors on your palette.

PREFACE TO THE EIGHTH EDITION

The eighth edition of *Introduction to Advocacy* contains expanded and newly updated material that we hope will make this book an even more effective guide to legal research, writing, and argument. While readers will find many changes throughout the book, we would like to highlight some of those changes here.

Much has changed since we published the seventh edition of this book in 2002. The way lawyers conduct legal research, for example, has evolved rapidly in recent years with the creation of new electronic research tools. In recognition of this fact, the eighth edition of *Introduction to Advocacy* focuses on introducing readers to the different types of sources they are likely to encounter and on helping them develop efficient and effective legal research strategies. No matter which of the many available research tools a reader uses, the legal research advice we provide in this edition should serve her well.

We are also pleased to announce the addition of a new chapter, Chapter 2, "Identifying and Synthesizing Rules." While students will likely receive significant training in how to read and find cases in law school, they must also learn how to use those cases to craft comprehensive rule statements for use in a memorandum or brief. Accordingly, this new chapter is designed to introduce readers to the types of rules they are likely to encounter, to help them find rules, to synthesize rules drawn from multiple authorities, and to evaluate the relative persuasiveness of those authorities.

In addition to these substantive changes, readers of the eighth edition will also find many significant updates. Along with a new sample predictive memorandum, we have added a sample assigning memorandum to reflect what students are likely to receive from their legal writing instructors or supervisors at their first legal job. We hope that providing students with both the assignment and the resulting memorandum will help add an element of realism and perspective to the materials. We have also updated both sample briefs, and our chapter on structuring legal analysis now models the more comprehensive CRuPAC structure, rather than the CRAC method described in the seventh edition.

ACKNOWLEDGMENTS

Introduction to Advocacy began as a pamphlet handed out to first-year students at Harvard Law School to help guide them through the school's required moot court program. It grew into a book forty-four years ago, and it has been revised seven times since then. For the past two years, the Harvard Law School's Board of Student Advisers (BSA) editing committee members have been hard at work, but we could not have made the new edition a reality without substantial help.

First, we would like to thank Adam Hornstine, a litigator at WilmerHale and BSA alumnus, for his incredible work revising and improving the sample briefs. We would also like to thank Ken Basin, an entertainment attorney and BSA alumnus who drafted the new assigning memorandum materials we are excited to include for the first time in this edition. Susannah Barton Tobin, Director of the First Year Legal Research and Writing Program, has our utmost gratitude not only for her feedback on this edition but also for her tireless work teaching countless students the skill and art of advocacy. Additionally, we would like to thank the research librarians of Harvard Law School who both taught us how to navigate the world of legal research and provided invaluable feedback on our legal research chapter. As always, BSA Administrative Coordinator Yvonne Smith has our deepest appreciation for everything she does for the BSA, and we would also like to thank the 2010–2011 and 2011–2012 BSA Executive Board members for their invaluable help and support. We sincerely appreciate the work everyone put into this edition.

Board of Student Advisers
ITA Editing Committee

Alisha Crovetto, Co-Chair
Joshua Sekoski, Co-Chair
Meredith Boak
Jeremy Bressman
Julienne Eby
Geoffrey Friedman
Claire Guehenno
Jeffrey Habenicht
Phillip Hill
Adam Hornstine
Michael Horrell
Tina Hwa
Wookie Kim
Melinda Kuritzky

SUMMARY OF CONTENTS

PREFACE III
PREFACE TO THE EIGHTH EDITION V
ACKNOWLEDGMENTS VII

PART I. PREDICTIVE WRITING

Chapter 1. Structuring Legal Writing: The CRuPAC Formula 3
I. Introduction 3
II. Using CRuPAC 3
III. A Final Note on the CRuPAC Formula 9

Chapter 2. Identifying and Synthesizing Rules 11
I. Introduction 11
II. Types of Rules 11
III. Hierarchy of Authority 12
IV. Finding the Rule 14
V. Synthesizing Rules 15

Chapter 3. Legal Research 19
I. Introduction 19
II. Where to Begin: Secondary Sources 20
III. Step Two: Primary Authorities 22
IV. Step Three: Shepardizing and Key Citing 24
V. When to Conclude Your Research 24

Chapter 4. Writing a Legal Research Memorandum 27
I. The Purpose of Memoranda 27
II. Parts of a Memorandum 28
III. Sample Memorandum: *Luke Baird v. Betsy Schmidt* (Internet Jurisdiction Case) 35

PART II. PERSUASIVE WRITING

Chapter 5. Approaching a Case and Developing a Core Theory 39
I. Facts in Context 39
II. Developing a Core Theory 40

Chapter 6. Writing a Brief 47
I. Introduction 47
II. Parts of a Brief 49
III. Sample Briefs: *Bell-Wesley v. O'Toole* 61

Chapter 7. Oral Arguments 63
I. Preparing for Oral Argument 63
II. Organizing the Oral Argument 67
III. Questions by the Court 70

IV. Presenting the Oral Argument 73
V. How to End Gracefully and Persuasively 75

Appendix A. Sample Assigning Materials 77

Appendix B. Sample Predictive Memorandum 89

Appendix C. Sample Record: *Bell-Wesley v. O'Toole* 101

Appendix D. Sample Appellant Brief: *Bell-Wesley v. O'Toole* 121

Appendix E. Sample Appellee Brief: *Bell-Wesley v. O'Toole* 137

TABLE OF CONTENTS

PREFACE III
PREFACE TO THE EIGHTH EDITION V
ACKNOWLEDGMENTS VII

PART I. PREDICTIVE WRITING

Chapter 1. Structuring Legal Writing: The CRuPAC Formula 3
I. Introduction 3
II. Using CRuPAC 3
    A. Leading with Your Conclusion 4
    B. Articulating the Rule 5
    C. Providing Proof of the Rule 5
    D. Application to Your Facts 6
    E. Reasserting Your Conclusion 8
III. A Final Note on the CRuPAC Formula 9

Chapter 2. Identifying and Synthesizing Rules 11
I. Introduction 11
II. Types of Rules 11
III. Hierarchy of Authority 12
    A. Binding versus Persuasive Authorities 12
    B. Evaluating Persuasive Authorities 13
IV. Finding the Rule 14
V. Synthesizing Rules 15

Chapter 3. Legal Research 19
I. Introduction 19
II. Where to Begin: Secondary Sources 20
    A. Legal Dictionaries 20
    B. Legal Encyclopedias 20
    C. *American Law Reports* 21
    D. Treatises 21
    E. Law Review Articles 21
    F. The Restatements of Law 22
III. Step Two: Primary Authorities 22
    A. Statutes 22
    B. Cases 23
IV. Step Three: Shepardizing and Key Citing 24
V. When to Conclude Your Research 24

Chapter 4. Writing a Legal Research Memorandum 27
I. The Purpose of Memoranda 27
II. Parts of a Memorandum 28
    A. Header 28
    B. Question(s) Presented 29
    C. Brief Answer 30

D. Statement of Facts 31
    1. Choose Only Relevant Facts 32
    2. Paraphrase When Appropriate 32
    3. Organize Your Facts 32
    4. Identify Holes in the Facts 32
    5. Cite the Source Materials 33
E. Applicable Statutes 33
F. Discussion 33
    1. Where to Begin 33
    2. Structure and Content 33
        a. Umbrella Section 33
        b. Headings 34
        c. Body Paragraphs 34
        d. Explanation of What You Omitted 34
        e. Use of Authority 34
G. Conclusion 35
III. Sample Memorandum: *Luke Baird v. Betsy Schmidt* (Internet Jurisdiction Case) 35

PART II. PERSUASIVE WRITING

Chapter 5. Approaching a Case and Developing a Core Theory 39
I. Facts in Context 39
II. Developing a Core Theory 40
    A. Read the Entire Record 41
    B. Create a Chronology or Diagram of What Happened 41
    C. Identify the Issues on Appeal and Begin Developing a Core Theory 41
    D. Determine the Standard of Review 42
    E. Connect the Facts to the Legal Issues 43
    F. Formulate Arguments 43
    G. Refine Your Core Theory 44
    H. Reread the Record, Consider Opposing Arguments and Core Theories, and Adjust Your Core Theory as Needed 44

Chapter 6. Writing a Brief 47
I. Introduction 47
    A. The Purpose of a Brief 47
    B. Rules of the Court 47
    C. Outlining 47
    D. Style 48
    E. Editing 48
    F. Convention 49
II. Parts of a Brief 49
    A. Title Page 49
    B. Table of Contents 49
    C. Table of Authorities 50
    D. Preliminary Statement 50
    E. Questions Presented 50

  1. Structure 51
  2. Substance 51
  3. Sample Questions 51
 F. Statement of Facts 52
  1. Choosing the Facts 53
  2. Using the Record 54
  3. Organizing the Facts 54
  4. Handling Adverse Facts 54
  5. Separating Fact from Argument 55
 G. Summary of the Argument 55
 H. Argument 55
  1. Argument Headings 56
  2. Subheadings 56
  3. Standard of Review 57
  4. Form of the Argument 58
  5. Substance of the Argument 58
  6. Preemption and Rebuttal of Arguments 59
  7. Arguing in the Alternative 60
 I. Conclusion 60
 J. Signature Block 60
III. Sample Briefs: *Bell-Wesley v. O'Toole* 61

Chapter 7. Oral Arguments 63
I. Preparing for Oral Argument 63
 A. Study the Record and Authorities 64
 B. Analyze the Arguments 64
  1. Use Your Core Theory 64
  2. Review and Prioritize Specific Arguments 65
 C. Strategy and Style 65
 D. Practice, Practice, Practice 66
II. Organizing the Oral Argument 67
 A. The Basic Structure of Oral Argument 67
  1. The Opening Statement 67
  2. Roadmap of Legal Arguments 68
  3. Statement of Facts 68
  4. The Arguments 69
  5. Conclusion 69
 B. Additional Considerations Specific to Each Party 69
  1. Appellee's Argument 69
  2. Appellant's Rebuttal 70
III. Questions by the Court 70
 A. The Value of Questions 70
 B. Effective Answering 71
  1. Be Responsive 71
  2. Advocate 71
  3. Be Sensitive to the Types of Questions Asked 72
 C. Questioning in Team Situations 73
IV. Presenting the Oral Argument 73
 A. Be Yourself 73
 B. Effective Delivery 73

  C. Attitude Toward the Court 74
  D. Handling Miscitations and Misrepresentations by Opposing
    Counsel 75
V. How to End Gracefully and Persuasively 75

Appendix A. Sample Assigning Materials 77

Appendix B. Sample Predictive Memorandum 89

Appendix C. Sample Record: *Bell-Wesley v. O'Toole* 101

Appendix D. Sample Appellant Brief: *Bell-Wesley v. O'Toole* 121

Appendix E. Sample Appellee Brief: *Bell-Wesley v. O'Toole* 137

UNIVERSITY CASEBOOK SERIES ®

INTRODUCTION TO ADVOCACY

RESEARCH, WRITING, AND ARGUMENT

EIGHTH EDITION

PART I

PREDICTIVE WRITING

In Part I of this book, you will learn the skills necessary to master predictive—or objective—legal writing. The goal of a predictive legal memorandum is, just as it sounds, to accurately and objectively predict a legal outcome. When a supervisor asks you to assess the likelihood of success of a particular case or argument, she is not asking you to advocate for one position or another. Rather, she is asking you to provide an objective determination of what result she can expect when existing law is applied to the facts of the case at hand. In this way, predictive legal writing is easily distinguishable from persuasive legal writing—a topic we will explore in Part II.

CHAPTER 1

STRUCTURING LEGAL WRITING: THE CRuPAC FORMULA

I. INTRODUCTION

During your years in law school, you will learn an incredible amount of information. Torts, civil procedure, contract law and many other subjects will occupy you for years. Becoming an effective lawyer, however, requires more than just knowledge of the law; in order to succeed in both school and practice, you must learn to write like a lawyer. The ability to explain your legal analysis clearly and persuasively to clients, coworkers, and judges is one of the most important skills you will develop as a young lawyer. Accordingly, this book is designed to help you develop the critical skills of legal advocacy.

In this chapter, we begin with the basic building block of legal writing: the paragraph. Each paragraph or section of your legal analysis should be designed to answer a specific question logically and effectively. Simply put, the goal is to apply the law to the facts of the case at hand and to arrive at a clear conclusion. The organizational method that we recommend here, called CRuPAC, is not the only way to structure legal analysis, but it is a useful tool of particular value to those students who are new to legal writing.

Although we will discuss using CRuPAC to organize a paragraph of legal analysis, keep in mind that a single CRuPAC may take the form of one or several paragraphs, depending on the complexity of the legal issue at hand. After all, good legal writing should still observe the basic tenets of good writing generally, and a paragraph should not be so long that it becomes unwieldy.

II. USING CRuPAC

CRuPAC is an acronym designed to reflect the basic structure of a section of legal writing.[1] It stands for Conclusion, Rule, Proof, Application, and Conclusion, and it is meant to provide a framework for your analysis of a legal issue. When crafting a section of legal analysis, first state your conclusion. Second, state the legal rule upon which you based you conclusion. Third, prove the rule by providing appropriate citation to legal authority. Fourth, apply the rule to the specific fact pattern that you are analyzing. Typically, this application will require you to compare the facts of your case to the facts of the case or cases from which you derived the

---

[1] The CRuPAC acronym suggested by Judith M. Stinson, Terrill Pollman, and Steve Epstein was popularized by Richard K. Neumann Jr. in LEGAL REASONING AND LEGAL WRITING: STRUCTURE, STRATEGY, AND STYLE (5th ed. 2005) at 100–03.

rule. Finally, you should close with a brief restatement of the legal conclusion that you articulated at the beginning of the paragraph.

A. Leading with Your Conclusion

Most novice legal writers follow a familiar pattern: first set out the legal and factual premises and then draw conclusions from them. The idea that a paragraph should begin with a conclusion may appear strange at first glance. However, busy attorneys, judges, and clients are pressed for time and do not want to hunt for your conclusion under layers of legal analysis. Therefore, legal writers should articulate their conclusions at the beginning of each paragraph or section.

Leading with a conclusion also requires you to think through the entire paragraph before you write the first sentence. Your conclusion should be a succinct statement of the result of your legal analysis. In a predictive memorandum, a conclusion statement predicts the likely legal resolution of a specific issue or explains how the law applies to the case at hand. Examples of both of these types of conclusion statements, taken from the Sample Memorandum in Appendix B, appear below:

> **Sample conclusion statements from a predictive memorandum:**
>
> "The court will probably find that Schmidt established minimum contacts with Illinois sufficient for the court to assert specific personal jurisdiction over her."
>
> "Schmidt's posting satisfies each prong of the <u>Calder</u> effects test."
>
> "Schmidt 'expressly aimed' the posting at Illinois."
>
> "Schmidt caused foreseeable harm to Baird in Illinois."
>
> (Sample Memorandum, Appendix B, pg. 92–98.)

Note the different types of conclusions in the examples above. The first conclusion answers the broad question of whether Schmidt has established sufficient "minimum contacts" with Illinois such that the exercise of personal jurisdiction over her is proper. This conclusion is appropriate because it is directly responsive to the question posed by the assigning attorney in this case. (*See* Assigning Materials, Appendix A, pg. 78.) The next three conclusion statements answer narrower sub-questions about whether particular elements or tests for establishing personal jurisdiction are satisfied. When you write your own conclusion statements, be sure that they are properly tailored to answer the legal issue or issues in question, however broad or narrow they may be.

Finally, it is sometimes helpful to know how *not* to begin a paragraph of legal analysis. Below are some common mistakes that beginning law students should work to avoid:

> **Common mistakes to avoid in conclusion statements:**
> - Stating a general principle of law without applying it to your case:
>   "The First Amendment to the U.S. Constitution guarantees the right to freedom of speech."

> - Describing the history of a legal principle:
>   "In Massachusetts, the exclusionary rule was first recognized in *Commonwealth v. Ford*."
> - Stating a central fact without rendering an opinion on its legal consequence:
>   "The accused did not intend to take the jacket from the store without paying for it."

Your conclusion sentence should connect the facts to the law. Each of the preceding three conclusions fails to do that, by omitting either the applicable law or the facts of the case at hand. A good leading sentence will make a conclusion about the connection between the two.

B. Articulating the Rule

Next, state the rule upon which you relied immediately after your conclusion. Often, your rule will be derived from cases that apply a relevant statute or that state an applicable common law principle. In the following example, the author of the Sample Memorandum concluded that "Schmidt caused foreseeable harm to Baird in Illinois." (Sample Memorandum, Appendix B, pg. 98.) To support this conclusion, the author provides a rule statement explaining how courts determine whether a defendant caused foreseeable harm in a state:

> **Sample Rule Statement:**
>
> **[Rule]:** In Illinois, to satisfy the third prong of the effects test, a defendant must cause harm to the plaintiff in Illinois that the defendant knows is likely to be suffered in Illinois.
>
> (Sample Memorandum, Appendix B, pg. 98.)

Note that the foreseeable harm rule here has two major requirements: 1) the defendant caused harm to the plaintiff in Illinois, and 2) the defendant knew that harm was likely to be suffered in Illinois. The author CRuPACs each element separately, and the remainder of this CRuPAC—as discussed in detail below—focuses on the first element of the foreseeability rule.

C. Providing Proof of the Rule

At a minimum, you must provide proof of your rule by citing the authority from which you took the rule. When providing a rule derived from a statute or opinion, you must cite the statute or opinion you used. This citation serves two very important functions: (1) it tells the reader that your rule is supported by legal authority and is not merely a product of your imagination, and (2) it allows the reader to evaluate the persuasiveness of the authority you cited when deciding whether or not to accept your conclusion. We will talk more about assessing the relative persuasiveness of authorities in Chapters 2 and 3.

While citation of a legal authority is always necessary, in many instances, it is not sufficient proof of a rule. Often, you should also provide a brief description of the relevant facts and disposition of the cited case or cases. Alternatively, you may need to include a detailed description of additional cases to explain sub-rules, exceptions, or a judicial gloss on the primary rule. In that case, the rule-proof component of your CRuPAC alone could span two or more paragraphs.

Merely providing a case citation as your proof of rule, unless the rule is both clear on its face and well-established, is usually inadequate for two reasons. First, without the facts and disposition, a holding is just words. Courts may say one thing and do another—showing *how* courts apply a legal principle to a set of facts is what gives that principle practical meaning. Second, without the facts, it is difficult to determine how the precedent cited may be applied to the facts of your case. Remember, however, that the proof should include only the facts relevant to the issue you are analyzing. Do not attempt to summarize all the facts of the case.

The Sample Memorandum in Appendix B provides many examples of detailed rule proofs. Building on the same sample CRuPAC analyzing foreseeable harm, note this time how the author provides extensive proof of the rule in the form of case citations and discussion of key facts and context:

> **Sample Proof of Rule:**
>
> **[Rule Proof]:** *Euromarket Designs, Inc. v. Crate & Barrel Ltd.*, 96 F. Supp. 2d 824, 835 (N.D. Ill. 2000). The court in *Jackson* found that the brunt of the harm from the allegations of steroid use did not occur in Jackson's home state because he had a national reputation. *See* 406 F. Supp. 2d at 896. The *Jackson* court distinguished *Calder*, noting that "because the entertainment industry of which [Jones] was a part was centered in California, she experienced the most severe harm in California." *Id.* Other jurisdictions have found that the brunt of the damage done to a plaintiff's personal (as opposed to professional) reputation occurs where she resides. *See, e.g., Zidon*, 344 F. Supp. 2d at 632.
>
> (Sample Memorandum, Appendix B, pg. 98.)

Note here that the author, after providing us with the general rule and a case citation to support it, then dives into the case law. She explains how the holdings from different cases and jurisdictions fit together to provide us with a more detailed understanding of the scope of the rule.

While the example above uses textual explanations of the relevant holdings, at other places in the Sample Memorandum, you will notice that the author uses parenthetical explanations of holdings in her rule proofs. (*See, e.g.*, Sample Memorandum, Appendix B, pg. 94–97.) Explanatory parentheticals can be an efficient and effective was to briefly summarize a relevant holding, but they are best used when a detailed comparison of the facts of the case with the one at hand is unnecessary. If a case requires significant discussion or if it is central to your analysis, you typically should not use a parenthetical to describe the case.

D. APPLICATION TO YOUR FACTS

Applying existing law to a new set of facts is one of the practicing lawyer's most important skills. In a legal memorandum or brief, this part of the analysis explains why the conclusion that was stated at the beginning of the paragraph or section is the correct one. Returning again to the Sample Memorandum in Appendix B, note how the author follows the proof of rule section by applying the rule to the facts at hand:

> **Sample Application Section:**
>
> [Application]: Baird specifically alleges that Schmidt's actions have caused him harm in Illinois by damaging his reputation, causing emotional distress, and impairing his earning capacity, see Compl. ¶¶ 35–37, allegations that the court will accept as true. Though Baird is seeking jobs nationally, has taken grants from foundations and the federal government, and has traveled frequently for business, Compl. ¶¶ 10–11, Schmidt Aff. ¶ 6, Schmidt will have difficulty convincing the court that Baird has a national reputation analogous to that of Jackson, who was a well-known professional athlete. However, even if the court accepts Schmidt's argument, Baird has nevertheless experienced "the most severe harm" in the forum where he lives and works. Baird's career and marriage are centered in Illinois. See Compl. ¶ 10. Because of the fallout from the posting, his wife forced him to move out of his Illinois home, Compl. ¶ 24, and his Illinois employer suspended him without pay, Compl. ¶ 27.
>
> (Sample Memorandum, Appendix B, pg. 99.)

The application section of the paragraph requires significant thought. You must compare and contrast the cases you cited with your own case. Argument by analogy to precedent, also called analogical reasoning, is a key tool in the lawyer's arsenal for predicting the outcome of a new set of facts under the law. To master this tool, you will need to explain how the facts at hand could lead to a similar outcome or how certain facts may distinguish your client's case from past cases, leading to a different outcome.

It is very important that you make your analogies explicit; do not expect your reader to connect the dots herself. Instead, tell your reader *exactly* how the cases you describe are similar to or different from the facts of your case. In the example above, note how the author directly contrasts Schmidt's experience with that of the plaintiff in the *Jackson* case. Below, you will find another example of analogical reasoning from the Sample Memorandum, this time focusing on comparing the evidence in Schmidt's case with the evidence in prior cases where Illinois was the "focal point" of the relevant online posting:

> **Another example of reasoning by analogy:**
>
> Schmidt exhibited a similar intent to "particularly and directly target" Illinois with her posting on lovehimorleavehim.com. Like the postings in *Miraglia* and *Zidon*, Schmidt's profile page makes clear that Illinois was the "focal point" of her statements. Schmidt's entire profile page was exclusively concerned with the conduct and reputation of an Illinois resident. *See* Baird Ex. A. Moreover, Schmidt's profile page mentioned numerous Illinois persons and places in addition to Baird, including the University of Chicago (Baird's employer in Illinois), Baird's wife (a resident of Illinois), and the Latin School (Baird's wife's employer in Illinois). *See* Baird Ex. A. Schmidt also listed Illinois as one of the relevant locations for her posting, *id.*, and users may search the profile

> pages on the website by their listed geographic locations, Compl. at ¶ 17.
>
> (Sample Memorandum, Appendix B, pg. 98.)

When reasoning by analogy, do not forget the importance of policy arguments. Just as you can compare or contrast the facts in previous cases with the facts in your case, you can also compare the applicability of underlying policy arguments. For example, imagine a court suggested in a prior opinion that its ruling on behalf of an injured employee was motivated in part by the desire to ensure swift and certain compensation for injured workers. If you represented an injured employee seeking workers' compensation, you would likely want to argue that the court's policy rationale in the earlier decision is equally applicable in your case. This skill is particularly important in instances where your research has not turned up any cases with facts similar to yours. At that point, your ability to analyze the central policy concerns in factually dissimilar cases in the same area of law, and to apply those policy concerns to your case, can make all the difference.

E. REASSERTING YOUR CONCLUSION

The basic unit of legal analysis ends with a short restatement of your conclusion. This statement will usually be shorter than the sentence with which you began the CRuPAC and it can often be more conclusory, although some writers prefer to reverse that order by providing shorter initial conclusions and more comprehensive final conclusions. In either case, the purpose of this conclusion is essentially to remind your reader what conclusion is properly drawn from the preceding application of the rule to the facts, and to signify that you have dealt with that particular issue and will be moving on to another issue in the next section.

Returning once more to the Sample Memorandum in Appendix B, we can now see the completed CRuPAC in its entirety.

> **Putting the CRuPAC Together:**
>
> **[Conclusion]:** Baird felt the brunt of the harm caused by Schmidt's posting in Illinois. **[Rule]:** In Illinois, to satisfy the third prong of the effects test, a defendant must cause harm to the plaintiff in Illinois that the defendant knows is likely to be suffered in Illinois. **[Rule Proof]:** *Euromarket Designs, Inc. v. Crate & Barrel Ltd.*, 96 F. Supp. 2d 824, 835 (N.D. Ill. 2000*)*. The court in *Jackson* found that the brunt of the harm from the allegations of steroid use did not occur in Jackson's home state because he had a national reputation. *See* 406 F. Supp. 2d at 896. The *Jackson* court distinguished *Calder*, noting that "because the entertainment industry of which [Jones] was a part was centered in California, she experienced the most severe harm in California." *Id.* Other jurisdictions have found that the brunt of the damage done to a plaintiff's personal (as opposed to professional) reputation occurs where she resides. *See, e.g., Zidon*, 344 F. Supp. 2d at 632.
>
> **[Application]:** Baird specifically alleges that Schmidt's actions have caused him harm in Illinois by damaging his reputation, causing emotional distress, and impairing his earning capacity, *see* Compl. ¶¶ 35–37, allegations that the court will accept as true.

> Though Baird is seeking jobs nationally, has taken grants from foundations and the federal government, and has traveled frequently for business, Compl. ¶¶ 10–11, Schmidt Aff. ¶ 6, Schmidt will have difficulty convincing the court that Baird has a national reputation analogous to that of Jackson, who was a well-known professional athlete. However, even if the court accepts Schmidt's argument, Baird has nevertheless experienced "the most severe harm" in the forum where he lives and works. Baird's career and marriage are centered in Illinois. See Compl. ¶ 10. Because of the fallout from the posting, his wife forced him to move out of his Illinois home, Compl. ¶ 24, and his Illinois employer suspended him without pay, Compl. ¶ 27. **[Conclusion]:** The Court will thus likely find that the primary effects of Schmidt's posting were felt in Illinois even if Schmidt's statements did harm Baird's job prospects across the country.
>
> (Sample Memorandum, Appendix B, pg. 98–99.)

III. A FINAL NOTE ON THE CRuPAC FORMULA

Although we refer to CRuPAC as a formula in this chapter, we do not mean to suggest that the elements of CRuPAC are inflexible. When looking at the Sample Memorandum in Appendix B, you may have noticed that some of the CRuPACs are significantly longer than others or are structured a little differently from one another. In a perfect world, legal issues would all be simple enough to fit each part of the CRuPAC in a single paragraph, in order. However, the law is rarely so simple, so do not be alarmed if your CRuPACs span multiple paragraphs in a section.

Always bear in mind that the purpose of legal writing is to communicate clearly to the reader your conclusions and analysis. We recommend CRuPAC as the best way to accomplish this goal, and your legal writing will benefit from its application. Although in time you may wish to deviate from the CRuPAC system, you must know the rules before you can break them. Mastering CRuPAC is well worth the effort.

CHAPTER 2

IDENTIFYING AND SYNTHESIZING RULES

I. INTRODUCTION

Rules are a common feature in all of our lives. The rules of the road tell us how to drive our cars. Rules of a game or sport define the limits of acceptable actions. Even mathematical and scientific formulas are rules that help us solve complex problems. In the legal world, a rule is a statement of the law on a given topic that, when applied to a set of facts, determines the legal result. In a way, legal rules are similar to mathematical formulas; they tell us what outcome a particular set of facts, or variables, should produce in the context of that rule or formula. If the facts satisfy the rule, then the legal outcome should be X. If the facts fail to satisfy the rule, then the legal outcome should be Y.

When a lawyer approaches a new set of facts, she must determine which legal rules are applicable to those facts before she can predict the likely outcome of the case or advocate effectively for her client. Through her research, she endeavors to find the relevant rule or set of rules within her jurisdiction that will control her case. The ability to take a case or series of cases and to derive a rule that you can apply to the facts at hand is one of the most important skills you will develop as a lawyer. Mastering the skill of rule synthesis also will pay dividends throughout your legal career.

This Chapter will give you the tools you need to pinpoint and define the rule from a case or set of cases. We first outline the different types of rules that you are likely to come across in your research. Next, we discuss the hierarchy of authority; that is, the relative persuasive value of different sources of rules. We then focus on finding the rule in a particular case. And finally, we walk through the process of synthesizing a rule statement from a collection of related case law.

II. TYPES OF RULES

In our judicial system, rules come from a variety of sources and take many forms. Federal and state constitutions, statutes, and regulations contain countless rules that courts must interpret. In addition, many rules in our common law system are judge-made and derive from prior judicial opinions.

A regulation prohibiting smoking within fifteen feet of a building is easy to understand and apply. Other more complex rules may have multiple elements, one or all of which must be satisfied in order for the rule to apply. For example, a theft statute might criminalize the taking of another's property *without* permission and *with* the intent of converting the property to the taker's use. In other words, you would need to establish both the absence of permission *and* the presence of intent to convert property to satisfy the statute. A vandalism statute, on the other hand, might criminalize defacing, damaging, *or* destroying someone else's property. A vandal could violate that statute in any one of three ways and still face prosecution.

Some of the most complex rules take the form of multi-factor tests and balancing tests. For example, a state court trying to determine whether a worker acted as an employee or an independent contractor at the time of her injury may apply a multi-factor test, considering such factors as the amount of skill required for the job, the length of time involved, the supplier of tools, the method of payment, and the beliefs of the parties. With multi-factor tests, typically no one factor is controlling and the court will look to the weight of the factors considered in context. Similarly, balancing tests ask the court to weigh one factor (or set of factors) against another to determine the correct legal outcome. In the due process context, for example, courts may need to weigh a defendant's interest in additional process against the burden that additional process might impose on the government.

No matter the type of rule you are dealing with, be alert to the possibility of exceptions. In a statute or regulation, watch out for critical words like "unless" or "except." Exceptions to common law rules may be less obvious, but a thorough search of the relevant jurisdiction's case law should reveal whether or not judges have developed any exceptions to the rule in question.

III. HIERARCHY OF AUTHORITY

A. BINDING VERSUS PERSUASIVE AUTHORITIES

In order to determine which rules will govern your case, you must pay careful attention to the source of the rule. "Binding" or "mandatory" authorities are those that all lower courts and administrative bodies in a jurisdiction must follow. For example, the United States Supreme Court's decisions on federal law are binding on all courts. "Persuasive" authorities may carry a great deal of weight because of the authoritativeness of the author, but a court need not follow them. For example, a judge sitting on the U.S. Court of Appeals for the First Circuit might find an opinion written by Judge Posner from the Seventh Circuit to be very persuasive, but the judge is not bound by an opinion from another circuit.

In the Sample Memorandum provided in Appendix B, the writer analyzes a personal jurisdiction issue for a case in the United States District Court for the Northern District of Illinois. Accordingly, she cites binding decisions from the U.S. Supreme Court and the Seventh Circuit Court of Appeals. In addition to these binding authorities, the writer also draws upon persuasive, factually similar cases from other jurisdictions, including the Fifth Circuit Court of Appeals and the United States District Court for the Northern District of Texas. Though persuasive, these cases do not bind the Northern District of Illinois, no matter how similar the fact patterns are.

The following paragraphs briefly outline which sources of case law are binding on the various levels of state and federal courts. Keep in mind that individual state rules may differ, so you should always double-check the rules of your jurisdiction before tackling your research.

State Courts: On matters of state law, lower state courts are bound by the decisions of the intermediate appellate court for their area (or all state intermediate courts, depending on the rules of the state) and the highest court of the state. Intermediate state courts are bound by the highest court of the state, but they are normally not bound by the decisions of other intermediate courts. The highest court of the state is bound only by its own precedent on questions of state law. This is known as the principle of *stare decisis*, which is a presumption against disturbing legal matters that have already been decided by the court. Of course, courts sometimes decline to follow *stare decisis* and instead choose to overrule outdated or poorly reasoned precedent. Finally, on issues of federal law, all state courts are bound by the decisions of the United States Supreme Court.

Federal Courts: On questions of federal law, federal district courts are bound by decisions of the court of appeals for the circuit in which they are found and by Supreme Court decisions. Federal courts of appeals are bound by the decisions of the United States Supreme Court and by their own past precedent under the principle of *stare decisis*. Federal district courts and courts of appeal may look to the decisions of other districts or circuits, but these are not binding. The Supreme Court is bound only by its own precedent under the principle of *stare decisis*. And when a federal court interprets state law—for example, in a civil suit with diversity jurisdiction—it is bound by the decisions of the highest court of the state in question.

B. Evaluating Persuasive Authorities

Even when an opinion with a favorable rule statement is not binding on your court, it may be useful as a persuasive authority. However, not all persuasive authorities are created equal. When deciding whether to bring a non-binding opinion to your reader's attention, you must keep in mind the hierarchy of authority, or the relative persuasiveness of a given source of law. Highly persuasive case law in a factually similar case may push a judge to accept your rule statement, while indiscriminate use of unpersuasive authorities may cause the court to question the strength of your research and analysis. Accordingly, learning how to evaluate the relative weight of the authorities you encounter is a critical part of learning how to find and compose well-supported rule statements.

Binding case law is of course the gold standard at the top of the hierarchy while unpersuasive authority is at the bottom. In order to determine the relative persuasiveness of non-binding authorities, consider the following factors:[1]

The identity of the issuing court: Even if the particular decision is not binding on your court, it is likely to carry more persuasive weight if it came from a higher source. For example, decisions of the federal Courts of Appeal can be very persuasive, even where they are not binding.

The date of the decision: Recent decisions are more persuasive than older decisions.

The power of the court's reasoning: Not all opinions are models of legal reasoning and writing. Well-thought out and well-argued decisions

---

[1] For a complete discussion of these and other factors relating to the relative persuasiveness of authorities, see LINDA H. EDWARDS, LEGAL WRITING: PROCESS, ANALYSIS, AND ORGANIZATION 61–63 (3rd ed. 2002).

are likely to be more persuasive than cursory and poorly supported opinions.

The centrality of the language to the holding: Legal reasoning that is used to determine the outcome of the case is more persuasive than a legal proposition mentioned only in passing or in a hypothetical. Words that are part of an opinion but not a necessary part of the court's holding are called *dicta* and have less persuasive value.

The number of judges: Unanimous opinions are more persuasive than divided opinions. When dealing with opinions with pluralities or with judges concurring or dissenting in part, be very careful that you understand the precedential value of the portion of the opinion you are using.

The subsequent treatment of the opinion: Some opinions are often cited in other decisions or in secondary sources. Opinions that are often cited may have strong persuasive value, even where they are not binding.

The reputation of the authoring judge: Some judges are highly respected, and opinions written by these judges may carry weight even if they are not binding.

IV. FINDING THE RULE

Once you've familiarized yourself with the different types of rules and the relative persuasiveness of their sources, the next step is to distill an explicit rule statement from those authorities that you can use in your analysis. Be sure not to confuse the rule, which is a generalizable principle that can be applied to other fact patterns, with the holding, which is specific to the facts of the case. If you are lucky, the opinions you use will state a rule explicitly and apply that rule in a straightforward manner. However, in many instances, you will be required to derive an implicit rule from the court's analysis. This section will focus on how to identify both explicit and implicit rules.

Explicit rules will often contain language signaling that the court is stating a rule. For example, the court will refer to the principle as a rule or a test, or will number the parts of the rule to clarify the definition. Explicit rules are, as expected, relatively easy to identify. Just be sure to read the opinion carefully so as not to be fooled by a statement that sounds like a rule statement but is not actually the rule the court is applying. If they are concisely written, explicit rules are also easy to quote for quick use in your CRuPAC rule statement.

Implicit rules, on the other hand, must be derived from an often-extensive discussion. As you read the case, you will have to pay close attention to the facts, the discussion, and the holding to determine the rule that the court is applying. Because you cannot excerpt the court's entire discussion in your CRuPAC, you will have to articulate your own version of the rule.

> **Example of an explicit rule:**
>
> "A three-pronged test has emerged for determining whether the exercise of specific personal jurisdiction over a non-resident defendant is appropriate: (1) the defendant must have sufficient 'minimum contacts' with the forum state, (2) the claim asserted against the defendant must arise out of those contacts, and (3) the exercise of jurisdiction must be reasonable."

> —*Zippo Mfg. Co. v. Zippo Dot Com, Inc.*, 952 F. Supp. 1119, 1122–23 (W.D. Pa. 1997).
>
> **Example of an implicit rule:**
>
> "The allegedly libelous story concerned the California activities of a California resident. It impugned the professionalism of an entertainer whose television career was centered in California. The article was drawn from California sources, and the brunt of the harm, in terms both of respondent's emotional distress and the injury to her professional reputation, was suffered in California. In sum, California is the focal point both of the story and of the harm suffered. Jurisdiction over petitioners is therefore proper in California based on the 'effects' of their Florida conduct in California."
>
> —*Calder v. Jones*, 465 U.S. 783, 788–89 (1984) (citations omitted).
>
> **Possible articulation of the implicit rule:**
>
> A state can properly exercise personal jurisdiction over a defendant where the defendant's allegedly tortious conduct was focused on that state and resulted in harmful effects in that state.

V. SYNTHESIZING RULES

Try as you might, it is not always possible to find a single case that clearly lays out the current state of the law on your issue. As a result, you may need to draw on multiple cases to get a full picture of the applicable law in your jurisdiction. Synthesizing a rule from multiple cases will require you to pay careful attention to the interplay between opinions. Is a later case refining the meaning of a rule in an earlier case or resolving a tension in the case law? Is it simplifying a rule or articulating a new one? In order to understand the legal landscape, you must know if an opinion is explicitly or implicitly overruling past case law or building on and refining a prior rule. Accordingly, you should pay careful attention to the dates the opinions were issued and the way in which they discuss prior case law.

Often, you will come across rules that each provide incomplete articulations of the law in your jurisdiction. In this situation, you must first determine if each rule is still good law by using a citator as described in Chapter Three. If you find that each of the complementary rules is still good law, your rule statement should reflect a complete statement of the law based on a combination of the rules. For example, imagine that Case A establishes a two-factor test, and Case B emphasizes two additional, different factors. In this situation, you will want to tell your reader first that different cases have emphasized a number of different factors, and then list those factors provided in the two cases. Note that a complete rule statement may require using more than one sentence and more than one citation.

In other instances, one case may provide an important judicial gloss on the rule of prior cases, perhaps expanding or narrowing an earlier rule. You will then need to synthesize a comprehensive rule statement using two or more cases.[2] Imagine that Case A says that in order to prove constructive eviction, a tenant must show that the landlord's actions had a

---

[2] For a detailed explanation of how to use inductive reasoning to synthesize rules, see TERESA J. REID RAMBO & LEANNE J. PFLAUM. LEGAL WRITING BY DESIGN: A GUIDE TO GREAT BRIEFS AND MEMOS § 2.9 (Carolina Academic Press ed., 2001).

permanent character. Case B held that two days was insufficient to prove permanence, and Case C held that two months was more than sufficient. A complete rule statement should identify the permanence requirement and explain that while the court has not specified the precise amount of time required, it is between two days and two months.

Sometimes, multiple cases that are binding on your client's case will have rules that seem to be in conflict. To make sense of the conflict, you need to know whether the tension signals that an earlier case was overruled or whether the outcome of the cases can be harmonized. Are the two different rules simply alternate ways of stating a similar proposition? Are the two cases distinguishable based on differences in the facts? Or was a policy concern that motivated the court's decision in the first case not applicable to the second?

The Sample Memorandum in Appendix B provides a good example of an instance where conflicting case law must be harmonized in order to create a complete rule. In the Memorandum, the author used her research skills to locate several Seventh Circuit cases interpreting the Supreme Court's *Calder* "Effects Test." However, the three main cases dealing with this issue include rule-like statements that are apparently in tension with one another. See if you can identify the potential tension(s) in the case law excerpted below.

Case excerpts seemingly in tension:

Wallace: The Supreme Court in *Calder* did not make the type of dramatic change in the due-process analysis of *in personam* jurisdiction advocated by the plaintiff. Rather, the so-called "effects" test is merely another way of assessing the defendant's relevant contacts with the forum State. The defendant must still "purposefully avail [himself] of the privilege of conducting activities within the forum State, thus invoking the benefits and protections of its laws." The forum State cannot hale the defendant into court "solely as a result of 'random,' 'fortuitous,' or 'attenuated' contacts." Jurisdiction is proper "where the contacts proximately result from actions by the defendant *himself* that create a 'substantial connection' with the forum State."

Indianapolis Colts: In *Calder* as in all the other cases that have come to our attention in which jurisdiction over a suit involving intellectual property (when broadly defined to include reputation, so that it includes *Calder* itself) was upheld, the defendant had done more than brought about an injury to an interest located in a particular state. The defendant had also "entered" the state in some fashion, as by the sale (in *Calder*) of the magazine containing the defamatory material. Well, we have that here too, because of the broadcasts, so we needn't decide whether the addition is indispensable.

Janmark: [T]here can be no serious doubt after *Calder* that the state in which the victim of a tort suffers the injury may entertain a suit against the accused tortfeasor. [*Indianapolis Colts*] applies this understanding to a case with many features in common with Janmark's. . . . Applying the principle that there is no tort without an injury, we held that the tort (if there was one) occurred in Indiana rather than Maryland. If operating a football team in Maryland can be a tort in Indiana, inducing the customers of an Illinois firm to drop their orders can be a tort in Illinois—and given 735 ILCS 5/2-209(c), whether or not it is a tort in Illinois, it is *actionable* in Illinois.

How would you describe the tensions among these three cases? *Wallace* seems to require something more than the basic Effects Test, in the form of a "substantial connection." *Indianapolis Colts* also states that some form of "entry" into the state may be a requirement for personal jurisdiction to be exercised. *Janmark*, on the other hand, suggests that the tortious effects of the defendant's act are enough to satisfy the requirements for personal jurisdiction. The following excerpt from the Sample Memorandum demonstrates one possibility for resolving this tension.

> **Synthesizing a rule from cases in tension:**
>
> On its face, the "entry" requirement of *Indianapolis Colts* appears to conflict with *Janmark*'s unqualified assertion that anyone who intentionally causes a tortious injury in Illinois is amenable to suit there. *See Caterpillar, Inc. v. Miskin Scraper Works, Inc.*, 256 F. Supp. 2d 849, 851–52 (C.D. Ill. 2003) (describing the tension between *Janmark* and *Indianapolis Colts*). However, since *Janmark*, district courts in the Seventh Circuit have resolved this linguistic discrepancy by equating the "entry" requirement of *Indianapolis Colts* with "express aiming." *See, e.g., id.* at 852; *Richter v. INSTAR Enters. Int'l*, 594 F. Supp. 2d 1000, 1010 (N.D. Ill. 2009); *Nerds on Call, Inc. v. Nerds on Call, Inc.*, 598 F.Supp.2d 913, 917, 919 (S.D. Ind. 2008).
>
> In other words, regardless of whether it is characterized as "entry" into the forum state or as "intentional and purposeful tortious conduct . . . calculated to cause injury in the forum state," *Caterpillar*, 256 F. Supp. 2d at 851, there must be some "express aiming" at the forum state in order for a court to assert personal jurisdiction over a non-resident tortfeasor. *See id.* Thus, despite the varying language used, courts in the Northern District of Illinois have all adopted some version of the traditional three-factor "effects test."
>
> (Sample Memorandum, Appendix B, pg. 95.)

In this example, the author was able to explain the relationship between seemingly contradictory case law in the first paragraph and to synthesize an appropriate rule statement in the second paragraph. She draws from useful persuasive authorities to highlight a trend in the case law and now, armed with her synthesized rule, she is ready to begin crafting a strong legal memorandum that will apply the relevant rule to the facts of her case.

CHAPTER 3

LEGAL RESEARCH

I. INTRODUCTION

Now that you understand how to structure legal analysis and craft rule statements, you are well on your way to becoming a skilled legal writer. Soon, you will likely receive your first legal writing assignment. Before you can begin writing, however, you will need to consult the appropriate legal authorities so that you can answer the legal question at issue. In some cases, your professor or supervisor will provide the relevant authorities for you, but most often, you will need to conduct your own legal research.

This short guide is designed to introduce you to the basics of legal research. It will provide an overview of several of the more useful types of sources available and suggest tips to make your legal research effective and efficient. Because technological developments are constantly changing the tools lawyers can use to find legal authorities, in this chapter we focus primarily on explaining the sources themselves rather than detailing the currently prevailing methods for locating the sources. For specific information about the legal research resources available to you and the preferred means of accessing them at your school or workplace, be sure to consult with a law librarian. No matter whether you use Westlaw, WestlawNext, Lexis, Lexis Advance, Bloomberg, or another research tool, the research practices outlined in this chapter should serve you well.

As an overview, the basic objective of legal research is to find the right binding, primary authorities to answer your question or to make your case. Primary authorities are those authorities that establish the law, like judicial opinions, constitutions, statutes, and regulations. Secondary authorities like legal dictionaries and treatises can prove very useful and may carry a great deal of weight, but unlike primary authorities, they explain rather than establish the law.

So how do you go about finding the right primary authorities? It may be tempting to dive right into a search of the relevant case law, but often the smartest research strategy is to begin by surveying secondary sources. Particularly when you are confronted with an unfamiliar area of the law, secondary sources like treatises, legal encyclopedias, and law review articles can help you find and understand the law. Not only will these sources reduce the time that you spend researching, but also the overview provided in secondary sources should help you understand the substance of primary sources more easily. Moreover, these secondary sources will often direct you to relevant primary sources and provide you with useful search terms. Keep in mind that legal publications are part of a large, interconnected system full of cross-references. There are many paths into this system, and once you have found one fruitful path, the others are readily accessible.

II. WHERE TO BEGIN: SECONDARY SOURCES

If the topic you are assigned is an unfamiliar one, getting a general sense of the substantive area of the research question before launching into a detailed search will save you time. Secondary sources like those discussed below will outline important issues and include specific legal terms that may help focus your search on the most relevant materials. They may also provide citations to seminal cases or statutes and help clarify which arguments courts and scholars focus on when addressing a particular question. A good secondary source may even highlight relevant controversies, tensions, and trends in the law.

Below is a brief introduction to the different types of secondary sources. Please note that the order in which we present secondary authorities here is not significant; different sources will prove more or less useful for different issues at different times in your research. Additionally, not all schools and employers offer access to the same resources, so be sure to consult with a law librarian to find out which secondary sources are available to you.

A. LEGAL DICTIONARIES

Imagine you just received a research assignment in an area you know nothing about. Before you begin researching in earnest, you will want to familiarize yourself with any new legal terms or principles. At this point, *Black's Legal Dictionary* is a useful tool and it is worth taking a moment to consult for two reasons. First, it will help you understand the legal terms of art you will be using, giving you confidence as you go forward. Second, many entries include citations to important cases that will help you later as you begin your case law research. For example, if you look up "sex discrimination" in *Black's*, you will find a citation to a landmark Supreme Court sex discrimination case, *Craig v. Boren*, 429 U.S. 190 (1970).

B. LEGAL ENCYCLOPEDIAS

Legal encyclopedias provide general discussions of virtually all legal subjects. The two most common encyclopedias are *Corpus Juris Secundum (C.J.S.)* and *American Jurisprudence 2d (Am. Jur. 2d)*, both produced by West Publishing. The national encyclopedias summarize the laws of all states and can provide a valuable, broad overview for a researcher new to a legal topic. One research tip is not to overlook the encyclopedias' tables of contents; when researching online, it can be tempting to type in keywords immediately, but browsing through the table of contents may give you more control over your search and a better understanding of the results.

If you are researching the law in a particular state, the broad overview a national legal encyclopedia provides may not contain enough detail about a given state's law to be helpful. There are also encyclopedias designed for individual states where the bar is large enough to sustain such a market. State legal encyclopedias offer helpful references to jurisdiction-specific cases and statutes, making them a very useful starting point for legal research.

C. AMERICAN LAW REPORTS

The *American Law Reports* (*ALR*) are an attorney-written, frequently updated series of annotated discussions about specific points of law. Most entries include a brief overview of a specific legal issue followed by an "annotation," or a synopsis of all American law on that narrow topic. Included, you will find citations to relevant cases, statutes, and law review articles. Because each ALR focuses on a very specific topic—for example, one entry focuses on the application of no-fault insurance to "school bus incidents"[1]—they do not cover every possible legal topic. That said, if you can find an on-point ALR, it should be a very helpful resource.

When you look at an ALR entry, expect to find a lengthy and detailed discussion of a relatively narrow legal issue; many entries go on for fifty or even a hundred pages or more. Thankfully, you will also find a detailed table of contents, a topical index, and a jurisdictional index that will allow you to quickly navigate the entry to find what you are looking for. The annotations also contain notes on parallel cases in other jurisdictions, which can be particularly helpful if the law in your jurisdiction is unsettled.

D. TREATISES

Treatises are scholarly publications that analyze a substantive area of the law with reference to case law and statutes. Many treatises are large, multi-volume texts, also available online via Westlaw or Lexis. For example, Wright and Miller's *Federal Practice and Procedure* is a massive, 31-volume analysis of the laws of federal criminal and civil procedure. Other treatises on more specialized topics, such as *Law of Asylum in the United States* by Deborah Anker, are but a single volume.

Still other treatises are targeted at law students rather than practitioners. These texts are more commonly known as "hornbooks," such as the *Examples & Explanations* series published by Aspen. Hornbooks can be useful introductory texts or serve as study guides for an exam, but they typically offer a general summary of the law rather than the kind of detailed analysis you will need for a legal research assignment. While it is perfectly appropriate for you to cite a well-respected treatise in a memorandum or brief, you should generally refrain from citing hornbooks.

E. LAW REVIEW ARTICLES

Law review articles can offer comprehensive perspectives on cutting-edge legal issues. Law reviews are periodicals typically produced at law schools and edited by students. They contain articles, student notes, case comments, and book reviews, and the authors are usually professors, judges, and students. In most cases, a law review article will provide a general discussion of the law in a specific subject area, a survey of law in one or more jurisdictions, or a more specific analysis of one important case. You can also expect most articles to advocate for the author's view about what the state of the law in an area is or should be. Law review articles are, by nature, extensively footnoted, which can make them a great source for finding citations to relevant primary sources. Because law reviews are published several times a year, they are one of the best sources for current debate on contemporary legal issues and trends.

---

[1] George L. Blum, *Application of Uninsured or Underinsured Motorist or No-Fault Insurance to School Bus Incidents*, 80 A.L.R.6th 389 (2012).

Most law reviews and journals are available in law libraries and electronically via Westlaw and Lexis. Additionally, you may have access to articles through a database like HeinOnline, via free internet resources like the Social Sciences Research Network (http://www.ssrn.com) and Google Scholar, or through indexes like the *Index to Legal Periodicals and Books* (*ILP*), the *Current Law Index* (*CLI*), or Legaltrac (also known as Legal Resource Index). These indexes catalogue articles by subject. Therefore, ILP, CLI, and Legaltrac can serve as efficient tools for finding the most relevant articles on a given topic. Note that article indexes do not always include the full text of the article, so you may need to use another resource like Westlaw or Lexis to access the full text of some articles. Different schools and employers will provide different resources for research, so be sure to familiarize yourself with the tools available to you.

F. THE RESTATEMENTS OF LAW

The Restatements of Law can also prove very helpful to a legal researcher. The Restatements of Law on common law topics are based on general trends in the development of the common law and are authored by committees of prominent scholars associated with the American Law Institute. The Restatements have achieved quasi-primary status in several substantive areas including agency, contracts, torts, property, trusts, judgments, and conflicts of laws. As a result, the Restatements are often cited in legal arguments and opinions, and many state courts have adopted the Restatements' articulation of common law as the law in their jurisdictions unless contrary to public policy.

Be aware that some Restatements have more than one version; thus, the *Restatement (Second) of Contracts* may more accurately reflect current law and thus be more authoritative than the original *Restatement of Contracts*. However, not all states are quick to adopt the most recent versions of Restatements, so be sure to refer the appropriate version for your jurisdiction.

III. STEP TWO: PRIMARY AUTHORITIES

A review of secondary sources for information on your research topic should have provided you with a sense of the contours of the law in that substantive area. In addition, these sources probably highlighted some of the key primary authorities that created legal standards and rules applicable to your research question. Now it is time to turn your attention to these primary authorities.

A. STATUTES

A good place to begin your primary authority research is by familiarizing yourself with the statutes you came across in your search of secondary authorities. Keep in mind that while a single statute may provide the answer to your research question, more often the issue you research will be presented as a unique, fact-specific situation. Therefore, your analysis will likely rely on the dynamic interaction between statutes and cases interpreting those statutes so that you can sufficiently address the specific facts presented. Because a statute could invalidate a long line of case law in one sweep, or a single opinion could change dramatically the way a statute is interpreted, thorough research is critical to determine which statutes—if any—actually govern your question. Also remember that statutes are frequently amended, so pay careful attention to the year of the code you consult to ensure that you use the current version of the statute.

When possible, utilize annotated statutes in your research. An annotated statute provides a list of primary and secondary authorities that reference that statute, which will be very useful when you begin to research case law. Both Westlaw and Lexis offer access to annotated federal and state statutes. Case annotations in Westlaw are called Notes of Decisions, and in Lexis they are called Interpretive Notes and Decisions. To familiarize yourself with annotated statutes, try looking up the Illinois long-arm statute analyzed in the Sample Memorandum at Appendix B: 735 Ill. Comp. Stat. 5/2-209(c) (2012). Though not identical, the annotated versions available on both Lexis and Westlaw provide notes for thousands of decisions interpreting the statute, arranged by subject and sortable by jurisdiction. This information will be very helpful as you move to the next step in your legal research: finding relevant case law.

B. CASES

Ideally, your secondary source search, along with any research you have done involving annotated statutes, pointed you in the direction of helpful leading cases. As you now turn to case law research, you will need to understand how cases are published in order to navigate them. Federal and state courts create case law by issuing opinions. Although the federal and state governments often publish cases, most opinions are made available today by commercial publishers. The chronological volumes in which decisions are published are called "reports" or "reporters."

Federal court cases are published in federal reporters. District court opinions appear in the *Federal Supplement* (F. Supp., F. Supp. 2d, and F. Supp. 3d), published by West. Opinions written by the federal courts of appeals are published in the *Federal Reporter* (F.), which is currently in its third numbered series, abbreviated in citation form as "F.3d." The official decisions of the Supreme Court of the United States are known as *United States Reports* (U.S.), while the West Publishing Company's version is known as the *Supreme Court Reporter* (S. Ct.) and the LexisNexis version is called the *U.S. Supreme Court Cases, Lawyers' Edition*. In the past, every state issued "official," i.e. governmentally published, reports of their highest court and sometimes of the intermediate appellate courts. Today, fewer than half of the states continue that practice, so the commercially published volumes are often the official state reporter.

So what should you expect to find when you read an opinion published by a commercial reporter service like Lexis or Westlaw? At the top of the document, you should see the case caption, which contains the names of the parties to the case. You will also see a case citation that identifies the reporter the opinion is published in, the volume in which the opinion appears, and the page on which the opinion starts. For example, the citation for *International Shoe Co. v. Washington* is 326 U.S. 310 (1945), which tells us that we have a Supreme Court opinion from 1945, published in volume 326 of the *United States Reports*, beginning on page 310.

Next, before the text of the opinion starts, you will find one or more paragraphs summarizing the key points of law in the opinion, organized by topic. These are called headnotes, and they are written by commercial editors, not by the court. While you should not cite headnotes, they are a useful research tool because they are indexed and searchable by topic and sub-topic. This indexing allows you to easily find other opinions that addressed the same point of law.

Finally, you may notice that some opinions say "unpublished" at the top of the page. Unpublished decisions are those opinions a court has chosen not to publish in a reporter. Commercial publishers like West, however, are free to disseminate these opinions, so you are likely to come across many of them in your research. Although the rules vary by jurisdiction, many courts do not recognize unpublished opinions as precedent and will limit or prohibit the citation of unpublished cases. While reading unpublished opinions can be educational and can direct you to additional, authoritative sources, you should check the rules of your court before including an unpublished case in a brief or motion.

IV. STEP THREE: SHEPARDIZING AND KEY CITING

Now that you have found useful primary authorities, the next step is to determine whether your authorities are still valid law. In other words, you want to verify that your cases have not been reversed on appeal, overruled by a later court, or limited by subsequent decisions or statutes. You also want to ensure that any statutes you cite are still in force. It is now time to consult a citator.

The two most commonly used citators are the Shepardize function on Lexis and the Key Cite function on Westlaw. When you use either citator, you will find lists of later opinions and secondary sources that refer to the case or statute that you are Shepardizing or Key Citing. Look out for any negative treatment of your authority and pay careful attention to its significance. For example, imagine you are researching in preparation for a federal trial in the District Court of Massachusetts. If you Key Cite an opinion from the District Court of Massachusetts and find that the First Circuit Court of Appeals later criticized the opinion and narrowed its holding, you should be cautious about relying on the District Court opinion. On the other hand, if the only negative treatment you find when you Key Cite the opinion is an opinion from a court in Florida that distinguished your case, you should feel comfortable relying on it.

Citators are also extremely useful as case-finding tools: once you have identified a source that is on point, a list of later cases that have cited your case may provide further insight, as well as more current articulations of the law. In addition to cases, you can use citators to chronicle treatment of the United States Constitution, federal and state statutes and regulations, and the Restatements of Law. Citators can also be used for law review articles: Key Cite an article to get a list of later primary and secondary sources that cite and possibly expand on the Key Cited article.

V. WHEN TO CONCLUDE YOUR RESEARCH

Because legal research often does not result in a simple and direct answer to your research question, knowing when to stop researching is one of the most difficult aspects of legal research. There are two general rules that offer some guidance.

First, when the sources you have found cross-reference each other without significant reliance on unfamiliar sources, you have probably found the most important sources. You may have noticed a cyclical feel to your legal research; a secondary source refers to a statute that leads you to a case, then another secondary source, then back to the first case. This fluidity is a natural part of exploring the interconnected, highly cross-referenced world of legal publications. The steps we outline in this chapter are meant to help you structure your approach to legal research, not to constrain you. Feel free to go back and forth between the steps suggested if that is where your research takes you. Eventually, you will start to see the same statutes and cases cited over and over again, and you can feel confident that you have fully researched your issue.

The second rule is framed in economic terms: when the marginal value of an additional source is less than the work required to access that source, stop researching. Over time, you will develop a sense of when you have done enough research. However, one hard-and-fast rule is to keep notes of your research strategy so that you or a colleague can retrace your steps efficiently if follow-up research is required.

CHAPTER 4

WRITING A LEGAL RESEARCH MEMORANDUM

I. THE PURPOSE OF MEMORANDA

Legal memoranda can serve a variety of purposes, but most often, they are designed for internal use within a firm or office. For example, when an attorney is deciding whether to take on a new client or case, she may first want a memorandum detailing possible claims and their likelihood of success in the relevant jurisdiction. At the appellate level, where the causes of action are already defined, an attorney may request a legal memorandum explaining the existing law on those causes of action. When it comes time to write a brief, that legal research memorandum will aid the attorney in efficiently and effectively presenting her case.

A legal memorandum of the type described in this Chapter is an explanatory, not persuasive, document. This characteristic distinguishes memorandums from briefs, described in Chapter 6, which require a writer to persuade readers that her client should prevail. In contrast, a predictive memorandum should present and evaluate arguments and their likely outcomes objectively.

In analyzing any given issue, a memorandum should identify the strongest and weakest points for both sides, including both the legal and policy arguments, regardless of which party is the client. When one side has tremendous support from case law and the other side far less, a good memorandum should make the imbalance clear to the reader. Likewise, the writer should point out any situations where precedent within the jurisdiction conflicts or where there is no binding authority (*see* Chapter 2, pg. 12 on the hierarchy of authority.) Furthermore, a predictive memorandum should candidly assess whether your client is likely to prevail or whether the desired outcome is likely to occur. After reading your memorandum, a reader should have a good sense of the applicable law in the given jurisdiction and how it is likely to apply to the case at hand.

If the memorandum is written at the appellate level, it provides the ideal foundation for writing a brief and preparing for oral argument. If the memorandum is written at the trial stage, it may help the attorney prepare preliminary filings and decide on a litigation strategy. For example, in the Sample Assigning Materials (*see* Appendix A, pg. 77), Betsy Schmidt's attorney is preparing for her defense and has requested a memorandum on whether the Illinois court's exercise of personal jurisdiction over Schmidt is proper.

The Sample Memorandum in Appendix B, however, is just one example of a legal memorandum. If your issue has been litigated often in your jurisdiction, you will likely have an abundance of relevant cases to use. The challenge will lie in distinguishing and analogizing between the cases and fact patterns effectively. On the other hand, if the case is one of first impression, you may need to draw analogies from dissimilar legal and factual scenarios and pay extra attention to policy arguments that both sides might use. Adjust your approach to meet the needs of the assignment.

Regardless of the approach, all good memoranda use the facts of the case to illustrate how the law operates in a particular arena. Good memoranda show how the facts of previous cases and the case at hand compare, drawing analogies between some facts and distinguishing others. As in all writing, clarity and simplicity are critical and can make the difference between an average memorandum and a great one. Keep sentences short and explain concepts clearly. Do not assume that your reader knows anything about your case or the causes of action involved.

Finally, it is important to listen carefully to the supervising attorney and ensure that you fully understand the parameters of your assignment. Law students and young lawyers often encounter difficulties because they misunderstand the scope of the assignment, not because they have trouble synthesizing the facts and the law. Get in the habit of asking questions and repeating the assignment back to your supervisor in order to prevent miscommunications.

II. PARTS OF A MEMORANDUM

The form of a memorandum differs depending on its purpose and the preferences of the person for whom it is written. The form described here is formal and comprehensive. But, particularly in an office setting, be sure to understand the format your supervisor wants and to tailor your memorandum accordingly. If you write a formal memorandum when instructed to send an e-mail of bullet points, you may waste valuable time and aggravate your assigning attorney.

Legal memoranda often contain the following sections:

A. Header;

B. Question(s) Presented;

C. Brief Answer(s);

D. Statement of Facts;

E. Applicable Statutes (optional);

F. Discussion; and

G. Conclusion

A detailed explanation of each section follows. Though the sections are discussed in the order in which they appear, note that you will probably not write the sections in this order. You should begin your memorandum by sketching out initial questions, conducting research, and outlining a structured discussion section. Once you have gone back and written out your discussion section, you will have a better grasp of your argument and can write a Statement of Facts section that incorporates all the relevant information. You will also be ready to tailor a specific question for the Question Presented section. Your last step will be to write the Brief Answer, which serves as a summary of the Discussion section, and your Conclusion.

A. HEADER

Memoranda begin by identifying the person for whom they are written, the author, the date, and the subject. In an intra-office memorandum, the subject should include the case name, a file number (if applicable), and topics covered by the memorandum. A comprehensive subject line will allow other attorneys in the office to find your memorandum easily when required, so do not overlook it. The date is also important because the precedential value of authorities often changes over time.

Before presenting a memorandum to your supervisor, you should learn the formatting style of your office. Pay special attention to which words are in bold or italic letters or are underlined, what information is included, and how many spaces should be between lines and sentences. Although it may seem trivial and superficial, many lawyers are very particular about the appearance of memoranda (see Sample Memorandum, Appendix B, pg. 89 for an example of a typical header).

B. QUESTION(S) PRESENTED

The Question Presented section performs two primary functions for the reader of the memorandum: (1) it informs the reader of the specific legal question arising from the facts of the case that the memorandum will answer, and (2) it establishes the organizational structure of the memorandum. When you present multiple questions to the reader, these questions should flow in a logical and coherent fashion. The memorandum should then answer the questions in the order in which they are presented.

Logistically, it is often helpful to write down a preliminary set of questions to help focus your research. Then, after the rest of the memorandum is complete, you can return to the Question Presented section to formulate one or more questions that clearly present the specific legal issues your Discussion section addresses. As a general rule, try to keep your Question Presented concise to maximize readability. Note that the number of questions is a matter of some discretion and will depend on the complexity of the issue discussed in the memorandum. For most memoranda, one to three questions will be sufficient. And if, as you formulate your questions, you find that the memorandum would be more effective with a different structure, do not be afraid to reorganize your Discussion section after developing the Questions Presented.

In its final form, your Question Presented should identify the jurisdiction for which you analyzed the law, incorporate the most important, legally relevant facts of the case you are evaluating, and be answerable in one or two words (i.e. "Yes," "No," "Probably Yes," or "Probably No"). To identify the most important, legally relevant facts, ask yourself which facts determine the legal outcome of the case. Resist the temptation to overburden your question with extraneous details that make it long and difficult to read. Above all, you question should be clear, complete, and concise.

For an example of a single, broad Question Presented, turn to the Sample Memorandum (*see* Sample Memorandum, Appendix B, pg. 89). Here, Betsy Schmidt's attorney wanted to file a motion to dismiss for lack of personal jurisdiction, and he asked the author to determine whether Schmidt established sufficient minimum contacts with Illinois:

> **Sample Question Presented:**
>
> Luke Baird, an Illinois resident, has filed a complaint against Betsy Schmidt in the Northern District of Illinois alleging defamation through a posting on lovehimorleavehim.com. In the posting, Schmidt accused Baird of conducting an extramarital affair while on business trips. The posting was forwarded via email to Baird's wife and employer in Illinois. By posting the accusation, has Schmidt established sufficient minimum contacts with Illinois such that the court may exercise personal jurisdiction over her?
>
> (Sample Memorandum, Appendix B, pg. 89.)

Note that the sample Question Presented is not one long, winding sentence, but rather a series of short concise, factual statements with a question posed at the end. In the past, many Questions Presented often took the form of a lengthy sentence, beginning with "whether" and ending with a lost reader who was unable to follow the countless clauses. Here, the example uses a modern approach consisting of multiple sentences; a quick introduction to the factual background is followed by a clear question. While this framing has the advantage of improved readability, be sure that you format your Question Presented with the individual preferences of your reader in mind.

C. Brief Answer

While this section precedes the Discussion section in your memorandum, you should write the Brief Answer after you have written your Discussion. This is because the Brief Answer is effectively a short summary of your Discussion and provides an answer to the Question Presented. Begin your Brief answer with a short sentence that answers the Question Presented: "Yes," "No," "Probably yes," or "Probably no." Then provide a succinct statement of the applicable law, and finally explain how the facts of your case fit into the law. With a few exceptions for cases establishing well-known tests, do not include references to specific cases—your reader can get citations and more detailed information from your Discussion section.

Remember that your Brief Answer should actually answer the Question Presented. After reading the Brief Answer, the reader should not need to search through the rest of the memorandum or have to make inferences to answer the legal question. Revealing the punch line up front might be a lousy way to tell a joke, but it is essential to writing an effective legal memorandum. Notice how the Brief Answer in the Sample Memorandum answers the Question Presented directly. Recall that the question was whether the defendant, Betsy Schmidt, had established sufficient minimum contacts with Illinois such that the exercise of personal jurisdiction over her was proper:

> **Sample Brief Answer:**
>
> Probably yes. Under the Due Process Clause as interpreted by the Supreme Court and the Seventh Circuit, a non-resident defendant establishes minimum contacts with a forum by committing an (1) intentional act which is (2) expressly aimed at the forum and (3) causes harm, the brunt of which is suffered—and which the defendant knows is likely to be suffered—in the forum. Schmidt's intentional posting of the statements is not in dispute, and she expressly aimed her actions at the forum by referencing Illinois in her posting, identifying Baird's Illinois employers, and inciting readers to contact Baird's wife. The court will presume that the harm has accrued in Illinois since that is where Baird resides. Because Schmidt knew that Baird lived and worked in Illinois and refused to remove the posting, she knew or should have known that her actions would likely harm Baird in Illinois. Thus, the court will likely find that Schmidt established minimum contacts with Illinois such that it is entitled to exercise personal jurisdiction over her.
>
> (Sample Memorandum, Appendix B, pg. 89.)

Notice that the brief answer above begins with "Probably yes." While it is a lawyer's job to determine how the law will be applied to a new fact pattern, it will not always be possible to answer your question with a definitive "yes" or a "no." Often, your client or supervisor asks you to predict the outcome of an issue that does not have an easy answer. Thus, at times, your Brief Answer might be a tempered "Probably yes" or "Probably no" with the understanding that you will explain in your Discussion why you have reached this conclusion.

After reading the Question Presented and the Brief Answer, the reader should know exactly what the memorandum covers and its conclusions. The structure of the memorandum should also be clear. For example, after reading the Question Presented and Brief Answer in the Sample Memorandum, we know that there are three main elements to determining whether Schmidt established sufficient minimum contacts such that Illinois could exercise personal jurisdiction over her. Moreover, we know the primary facts that the memorandum will address for each prong and the order in which they will be discussed.

D. STATEMENT OF FACTS

In the Statement of Facts section, you should tell the reader—in narrative form—all of the facts that will be relevant to the analysis in your Discussion section. This should also include procedural facts that tell your reader what stage of litigation you are currently in and how you got there. Remember that in a memorandum, you must be objective in your presentation, so try to avoid slanting or unnecessarily characterizing the facts. For example, an appropriate sentence might say "John Doe fell down the stairs and broke his foot," but not "John Doe stumbled down the dilapidated, negligently constructed stairs and tragically broke his foot."

Additionally, even if the person who has given you the assignment knows the facts well, write this section as though the reader were unfamiliar with the case unless you are told to do otherwise. Your supervisor may pass along your memorandum to another reader who will need to know the facts.

Keep the following tips in mind when writing your Statement of Facts:

1. Choose Only Relevant Facts

Weak fact patterns often contain more detail than necessary. Present only those facts that are relevant to your legal analysis or necessary to give your reader a clear picture of what happened. Remember, however, that your memorandum will anticipate potential arguments for opposing counsel. Thus, the facts relevant to both sides' arguments must be included in your Statement of Facts; do not confuse or blindside a reader by burying an essential fact in your Discussion section.

2. Paraphrase When Appropriate

Generally, you should select and paraphrase the relevant facts from the record because often the fact pattern or record (if the memorandum is being written at the appellate stage) will contain confusing and unnecessary details. Remember, however, that you must present the facts coherently, and thus at times it will be preferable simply to quote from the record. For example, in the Sample Memorandum, rather than trying to explain to the reader the kind of information Schmidt posted on the Internet, the author directly quoted Schmidt's posts. (*See* Appendix B, pgs. 90–91.) The author also did a good job of summarizing the website's purpose to convey concisely to the reader the type of online source at issue. (*See* Sample Memorandum, Appendix B, pg. 90.) When it is time for you to write your Statement of Facts, think critically about the principles of clarity and concision when deciding whether paraphrasing or a direct quotation will serve you best.

3. Organize Your Facts

While you need not always structure your facts in chronological order, that is often the clearest way to present the material. Another way to organize the section is to begin with the facts most important to your analysis and to then explain the events that led up to them. Note that the Sample Memorandum's Statement of Facts, for example, begins with Schmidt's posting about Baird. It then fills the reader in on the facts leading up to that action—Schmidt and Baird's relationship, information about the identities of the parties, etc. (*See* Sample Memorandum, Appendix B, pgs. 90–91.) This emphasizes the key action at issue: Schmidt's Internet posting that led to Baird's defamation lawsuit. In addition to presenting your facts in chronological order, you can also emphasize the most important facts by placing them in more prominent positions throughout the narrative, such as at the beginning of a paragraph.

4. Identify Holes in the Facts

After analyzing the elements of the legal issue, you may realize that there are holes in the facts that leave some questions unanswered. Nevertheless, in piecing facts together, you may be able to draw logical inferences. These inferences can and should be identified and used in the Discussion section when you apply the law to your facts. However, in the Statement of Facts, you should only note the absence of a fact that will later be central to the analysis and, if possible, the reason why that fact is missing (e.g., a key witness has not yet been deposed).

5. Cite the Source Materials

Readers must be able to find the sources for the facts that you include, as paraphrases or direct quotations, in your Statement of Facts. When the memorandum assignment is at the trial stage, students should cite directly to source materials throughout the Statement of Facts section. If the memorandum is being written at the appellate stage, the author of the memorandum should cite the record. The Bluebook contains rules for citing to various legal and non-legal documents, so be sure to consult it when formatting your citations.

E. Applicable Statutes

If statutes or other regulations govern the legal issues you identify, your reader needs to be aware of the relevant parts of the statutes or regulations. You may want to include these provisions in a separate section of the memorandum. If only a small part of a statute or regulation applies, including that part in the text of your memorandum or in a footnote may suffice. As always, let your best judgment and the preferences of your assigning attorney or instructor be your guide.

F. Discussion

The goal of the Discussion section is to analyze the issues relevant to answering your Question Presented. Present your relevant findings and your analysis of them in a straightforward, detailed, and structured manner. Remember to structure your analysis according to the CRuPAC formula. (*See* Chapter 1, pg. 3.) After reading the Discussion section, your reader should be familiar with the relevant law on the issues discussed and with how a court in your jurisdiction would likely rule on each issue.

1. Where to Begin

Begin by creating an outline. It can be tempting to dive right in, but you will have a number of cases, issues, and ideas to address by the time you complete your research. You do yourself a disservice if you begin writing without taking the time to think about how best to present them in a logical, organized fashion. Think about how the components of your analysis relate to each other and how they flow best. At this point, the CRuPAC structure will help you group statutes and cases that you will use for your Rule and Proof sections for each issue. Finally, do not forget to include counterarguments in your outline.

2. Structure and Content

Your arguments should follow logically from one to the next. The following tools should help you make your structure clear to your reader:

a. Umbrella Section

Include a paragraph or two in the beginning of your Discussion Section to outline the overarching rules and preview the primary conclusions of your memorandum. This paragraph may feel repetitive to you after writing the Brief Answer and Question Presented, but it provides further road-mapping for your reader to understand how the Discussion section will proceed. An umbrella paragraph is particularly useful for memoranda that deal with lengthy or complicated questions that require the explication of many rules and sub-rules.

b. Headings

If you are analyzing multiple issues, separate sections for each issue will help your reader follow the logical structure of the Discussion. You create these sections by using headings and sub-headings, which are a great tool to help organize complex legal issues. A typical, strong heading should be a full sentence, without a period at the end, that states your conclusion for that section. In the Sample Memorandum, for example, the first heading states, "The Northern District of Illinois has interpreted potentially inconsistent Seventh Circuit precedent as requiring a defendant to satisfy all three prongs of the *Calder* effects test." (*See* Appendix B, pg. 93.) The second main heading states, "Schmidt's posting satisfies each prong of the *Calder* effects test," and the author uses subheadings to explain separately how Schmidt satisfies each prong. (*See* Sample Memorandum, Appendix B, pg. 95.) To determine whether your headings are effective, imagine that your busy supervisor has only a minute to glance through your memorandum and will only read the headings and subheadings in your Discussion section. If she can understand the flow of your argument and grasp your conclusions, your headings are in good shape. If you are tight on space, also keep in mind that headings may also serve as the initial conclusion statement for each of your CRuPACs.

c. Body Paragraphs

The body paragraphs of your Discussion section are the "meat" of your argument. In these paragraphs, you will use the CRuPAC method to "prove" the conclusion in the heading. Depending on the law or facts with which you are working, you may need a whole paragraph to discuss just one or two elements of CRuPAC. For example, in Part II.C.i. of the Sample Memorandum (*see* Appendix B, pg. 98), the author stated the "rule" and "proof" in the first paragraph of the section, went through the "application" in the second paragraph of the section, and ended with a "conclusion." For a more in-depth discussion of how CRuPAC will operate within your Discussion section, review Chapter 1.

d. Explanation of What You Omitted

If you are writing a memorandum for a long-term project in which others may expand upon your work, you may want to include a paragraph at the end of your Discussion section explaining potential claims you have already researched and eliminated or flagging areas for further research. You could also create a separate section containing this information. This may facilitate the work of someone coming after you on the same project.

e. Use of Authority

When choosing which cases to cite in your Discussion, select those with the greatest relevance and the greatest weight. Review Chapter 2's explanation of binding and persuasive authority to determine which authorities you will want to use. (*See* Chapter 2, pg. 12.) Be sure to use proper citations and to format them according to the rules of your court.

G. Conclusion

Include a brief summary of your conclusions in this section similar to, though not identical to, your Brief Answer (your reader can always look at your Brief Answer again; this is an opportunity to present your conclusions in a new way). As in the Brief Answer, do not cite authorities here, but merely set forth your conclusions. The Conclusion section should be very short—no more than a few lines.

III. Sample Memorandum: *Luke Baird v. Betsy Schmidt* (Internet Jurisdiction Case)

A sample memorandum evaluating a potential defense for Betsy Schmidt in a defamation lawsuit filed by Luke Baird is located in Appendix B, beginning on page 89. The memorandum evaluates whether an Illinois court's exercise of personal jurisdiction over Schmidt is proper, presents the policy and case law arguments, and suggests ways in which the argument might be approached from both sides. With this Chapter fresh in your mind, read through the Sample Memorandum now to get a better idea of what these tips and tools look like in practice.

PART II

PERSUASIVE WRITING

In Part II of this book, we turn our attention from predictive writing to the art of persuasion. In the pages that follow, you will learn how to become an effective advocate for your client. You will discover how to approach a case, how to develop a core theory of the case, how to write a brief, and how to argue on your clients' behalf. The fundamentals you learned in Part I—organization, rule synthesis, and legal research—continue to apply, but you will now use those skills in a different context. As you turn the page, remember that your goal is no longer objectivity; your new objective is advocacy.

CHAPTER 5

APPROACHING A CASE AND DEVELOPING A CORE THEORY

At their core, lawyers are advocates for their clients. When a lawyer takes on a client's case, she must persuade a neutral third party that the client is in the right. Thus, the ability to write persuasively is one of the most important skills that a lawyer can develop. Before you can begin writing an effective and persuasive brief, however, you must learn how to approach a case and develop a core theory.

A core theory, or theory of the case, is central to the persuasiveness of a brief. A core theory is a concise theme or story that weaves together the favorable legal, factual, and policy elements at play in the case. A strong core theory will motivate the court to find for your side.

Core theory can be a difficult concept to grasp, because law students and young lawyers often want to make arguments based solely on the legal standards they found during their research. However, your experiences in other first-year classes should illustrate the importance of core theory. First-year law students quickly discover that very similar facts applied to the same legal standard can, at times, lead to radically different outcomes. It is often the core theory of a case—the policy considerations, factual distinctions, and sometimes simple common sense—that drives judges' decisions. Therefore, development of a core theory that is compelling, logical, and appealing is one of the most important parts of legal advocacy.

I. FACTS IN CONTEXT

Facts can lend themselves to more than one interpretation. It is your job to examine the facts critically to discover which ones are important to your case. A strong presentation of the facts, with effective organization and the appropriate tone, will help persuade the court to view the case from your perspective.

For example, consider the fairy tale of *Goldilocks and the Three Bears*. From the bears' perspective, the important facts are that they came home to find their house a wreck, their food eaten, and a potentially dangerous intruder passed out in their bedroom—an open and shut case for breaking and entering, robbery, and trespass. From Goldilocks's perspective, she was lost, starving, and could barely make it to the door of the bears' home. To avoid starvation, she entered the house, ate some porridge, and passed out in a bed only to be terrified by the arrival of angry bears. She had no malicious intentions and only did what she needed to survive. Creating a cohesive story is central to developing a strong core theory. For the bears, the story was of a grievous violation to the sanctity of their home by a shameless stranger. For Goldilocks, the story was one of fear, desperation, and necessity.

As you review your case, try to view the facts from different perspectives. In order to make a compelling argument, you need to develop an appropriate and credible narrative that will inform your core theory. In

Bell-Wesley v. O'Toole, Rebecca Bell-Wesley gave birth to a healthy baby boy, Frank. Dr. O'Toole viewed the birth as a benefit to the Bell-Wesleys, who had tried unsuccessfully to conceive a healthy child over a period of years. For the Bell-Wesleys, however, the conception and birth of their son violated a conscious choice they had made to forego having children and irrevocably changed their lives. These alternate views of Frank's birth will influence the way each side addresses the legal issues.

Finally, remember that this process is dynamic. Your understanding of the facts will often change, sometimes radically, over the course of the research and writing process. A clear understanding of the facts is always essential, but the context and importance of many of the facts will be influenced by your research and by reflection on your core theory. In other words, the relevance of otherwise-favorable facts will largely depend on the core theory that you present. Be prepared to re-evaluate your interpretation of the facts in order to make the strongest arguments for your client.

II. DEVELOPING A CORE THEORY

Work on the core theory begins upon initial review of the facts and continues throughout the process of legal research and writing. Consider first the non-legal reasons that justify a decision in your favor, such as policy implications or factual distinctions. Many times, other cases discussing your issue will address such considerations. Then, as you research, incorporate the law into your core theory. The legal aspect of your core theory is important for two reasons: it constrains the policy and other arguments that you can make, and it becomes in itself a part of the story that you tell.

Developing a core theory takes time and thought. As you review the record and your research, try to structure your ideas around a theory that captures the essence of your case. Next, try articulating your core theory into a narrative of several words or sentences. It is a challenging step, but the process of distilling your ideas into a few sentences ultimately will produce the strand that connects your ideas into a cohesive whole. Note that in many cases, you may not want to write your theory verbatim into your brief; rather than use your theory explicitly, it is often more effective to incorporate it implicitly, using it as an internal guidepost to orient you as weave together the facts, law, and policy into a compelling narrative.

When you first receive an assignment to write a brief, you may wonder where to begin and how to approach your case and develop a core theory. The following list of tasks, explained in more detail below, will help direct and focus your work:

A. Read the entire record.

B. Create a chronology or diagram of what happened.

C. Identify the issues on appeal and begin developing a core theory.

D. Determine and consider the standard of review.

E. Connect the facts to the legal issues.

F. Formulate arguments.

G. Refine your core theory.

H. Reread the record, consider opposing arguments and core theories, and adjust your core theory as needed.

A. Read the Entire Record

An initial review of the entire record will help you understand what is happening both legally and factually. Your job on appeal is to examine the lower court's decision closely to determine the precise legal grounds for the opinion, the potential issues of reversible error, and the available arguments for your position. Because the record is your only source of factual information, a mastery of the record is a prerequisite to an effective appeal.

As you read the record, be aware of the varying importance different courts will attach to different types of facts. Typically, the appellate court will give the greatest weight to the lower court's findings of fact. Remember also that the extent to which the appellate court defers to the lower court's findings of fact depends on the standard of review.

A comprehensive understanding of the record will also facilitate the initial stages of your research and help you plot a logical course of action. By rushing to research without carefully considering the intricacies and nuances that inevitably exist in the record, you may find yourself exploring many unproductive or irrelevant paths. Your research will be more efficient and effective from the outset if you begin with a solid understanding of the case.

B. Create a Chronology or Diagram of What Happened

The items in a record are not necessarily arranged in the order in which events actually happened. By preparing a chronology of events, you will have a comprehensive understanding of the factual setting. This is important because many cases depend equally on what happened and when it happened.

For example, in *Bell-Wesley v. O'Toole*, one of the important issues is whether Frank's birth harmed Rebecca Bell-Wesley's career goals. You need to examine the trial record of Rebecca's testimony to learn about her potential lost career opportunities. A reading of the record shows that Rebecca became pregnant after she accepted a new position at the attorney general's office. This is very important, because if Rebecca had become pregnant before she accepted the new position, she would be less likely to succeed in her claim for damages.

In any court record, some facts will be missing or ambiguous. Once you notice which relevant facts are missing, look more closely at the record to see if these facts are hidden or if they can be reasonably inferred from available facts. Facts inferred from the record should become a part of your argument. If you choose to include them in the Statement of Facts, however, be sure to preface them in a way that signals to the court that you are making an inference. The misuse of facts or the use of inference as undisputed fact will reduce your credibility with the court.

C. Identify the Issues on Appeal and Begin Developing a Core Theory

On appeal, the legal issues are narrower and more defined than at the trial court level. At the trial level, both parties raise all the legal issues they think are at stake, but at the appellate level, the court certifies only particular questions of law for appeal. It is very important that both parties brief only those issues within the scope of the appeal. For example, the court certified a question on the last page of the *Bell-Wesley v. O'Toole* record telling the parties to focus on the issue of whether the cost of raising a child should be included in the damages calculation for a wrongful pregnancy action. (*See* Appendix C, pg. 120.) This tells the parties that they need not and should not raise the possible negligence arguments concerning the vasectomy, as that issue is beyond the scope of the appeal.

The best places to discover the relevant legal and factual issues on appeal are in the lower court opinion and in the certified questions. They discuss the reasons for the court's ruling and frame the issues for appeal. In *Bell-Wesley v. O'Toole*, the judge's fifth and sixth conclusions of law point you to the two vital issues on appeal: can the court award damages for a wrongful pregnancy, and what items should enter into the calculation of these damages? (*See* Record, Appendix C, pg. 113.)

In other cases, the opinion and record will not frame the issues so clearly, but a careful reading of the relevant documents should provide you with the important legal issues for the appeal. In non-moot-court contexts, the narrowing of the issues may be considerably more difficult and may itself require a significant amount of legal research. In that case, be sure that you are selective when choosing the issues for appeal. If you think you have nine different grounds for appeal, you are often served best by selecting and focusing only on your strongest handful of arguments so as not to dilute the strength of your appeal.

In narrowing the issues, you will also be presented with policy implications that should prompt refinement of your core theory. *Bell-Wesley v. O'Toole* presents several policy issues:

- Should society allow parents who keep a child to force the doctor who negligently performed a vasectomy to pay for all of the costs incurred in raising a child?
- What impact would such payment have on a child?
- What impact would such payment have on the medical profession?
- What impact would such a payment have on other potential plaintiffs and defendants in a similar situation?
- Would a decision against the doctor make it more difficult for patients to find other doctors willing to perform a sterilization procedure?
- Should the court be concerned about the possible expressive function of an order treating a child's healthy birth and life as a cause for damages?

You need not, and probably cannot, determine all of the legal and policy issues presented by the case before beginning your research. Indeed, in the course of your research, you should continuously refine issues and consider new ways of looking at the case. Legal research is a dynamic process of defining issues, developing arguments, and finding support for those arguments.

D. Determine the Standard of Review

When a higher court reviews a lower court's ruling, the standard of review defines the extent of the actions that the appellate court can take with respect to the issues before it, as well as the deference it must give the lower court's decisions. In some instances, the standard of review will be mentioned in the record. When the standard of review is not stipulated, you should research it as you would any other legal issue.

Potential standards of review range from "de novo" review to "abuse of discretion" or "clearly erroneous" review. An appellate court nearly always reviews conclusions of law de novo, which means that it shows no deference to the lower court's decision and reviews the legal issues as if they were being considered for the first time. Findings of fact are often reviewed for clear error, which means that the appellate court does not disturb the lower court's decision unless it strongly believes the lower court clearly made a mistake. Thus, it is important to distinguish the lower court's legal findings from its factual findings.

The standard of review will have implications for both your written and oral advocacy. For example, if you are arguing that there was an abuse of discretion at the trial court level, you likely will want to focus your arguments on the facts. On the other hand, if the court is reviewing an question of law de novo, you may wish to spend more time arguing the relevant law.

E. CONNECT THE FACTS TO THE LEGAL ISSUES

By this point, you will have a solid grasp of what actually happened and of the legal considerations. You should begin to synthesize the two sets of information. The key to an effective argument is your ability to relate the legal arguments to the specific factual situation. This synthesis requires you to look critically at the information in the record to determine which facts matter the most to your arguments. In the *Bell-Wesley* case, not every fact concerning Dr. O'Toole's performance of the vasectomy is relevant. The important facts for the appellants are those that demonstrate how the wrongful pregnancy of a child can be a real injury to the parents. For example, evidence of the economic and emotional costs to Rebecca and Scott Bell-Wesley can be used for this purpose.

Highlight these important facts when making your legal argument. The best arguments not only state the relevant law persuasively and accurately, but also show how the facts of the present case fit the law. The stronger your connection of the facts to the law, the more persuasive your brief will be.

The process of relating the facts to the law helps you continually redefine the factual and legal issues. There is a symbiosis between the facts and the legal issues. The important facts are determined by the legal issues, and the legal issues are determined by the facts of the case. Neither can be evaluated in a vacuum and both must be considered and reconsidered in light of the core theory.

F. FORMULATE ARGUMENTS

The arguments you make in your written and oral presentation to the court answer the questions raised in your case and stated in the "Questions Presented" section of your brief, which we will discuss in more detail in the next Chapter. These arguments are the reasons the court should find in your favor. Formulating arguments is a process, involving analysis of precedent and analogical reasoning. You should prepare arguments in conjunction with your development of a core theory, as a strong core theory will link all parts of your legal argument together into a cohesive and compelling whole.

Do not be afraid to rely on your intuition. If you had to explain to a parent or friend why you think your client should win, what would you say? Begin thinking about how you can best frame the arguments for (and against) the position you wish to support. Consider also the following list of types of arguments to help you generate ideas:

- Arguments based on common-sense notions of justice and equity;
- Arguments based on authorities and case law that you have already studied;
- Arguments by analogy or comparison to other cases and situations with which you are familiar;
- Arguments typically associated with the subject matter of the case;
- Arguments based on the potential consequences of the court's decision; and
- Arguments drawing upon public policy.

This list is a starting point. During the course of your research, you will discover new arguments to add to the list and reject some as frivolous. As you can see, many of the argument considerations are also those that drive the core theory.

G. REFINE YOUR CORE THEORY

After identifying the legal, factual, and policy issues and generating a series of useful arguments, try to unite them into a core theory. Any case can give rise to a number of alternative core theories. Here are some examples of what a core theory could look like for the appellant and appellee in *Bell-Wesley v. O'Toole*:

> **Sample Core Theories:**
>
> *Appellant:* The Bell-Wesleys' wrongful pregnancy claim is indistinguishable from any other medical malpractice claim. They must be compensated for all of the injuries flowing from Dr. O'Toole's repeated negligence, and that includes the substantial cost of raising a child to adulthood.
>
> *Appellee:* The Bell-Wesleys wanted a healthy child and they got one. Rather than being injured by their son's birth, the Bell-Wesleys benefited from it, as would any parents fortunate enough to have a healthy child in our society.

H. REREAD THE RECORD, CONSIDER OPPOSING ARGUMENTS AND CORE THEORIES, AND ADJUST YOUR CORE THEORY AS NEEDED

Anticipating the opposing side's arguments gives you a window into your opponent's mind and an opportunity to identify weaknesses in your own arguments and core theory. How you use your opponent's arguments in your brief is part strategy and part personal preference. At this stage, however, you should strive to brainstorm all of the other side's best theories and arguments.

Next, consider whether you want to make changes to your core theory in response to your opponent's likely arguments. Imagine you are a defense attorney and that you are defending a teacher who you believe was wrongly accused of assaulting a child. You might be tempted to build your defense around the theory that the crime is incompatible with your client's nature; he is a respected teacher who has dedicated years of his life to educating children and would never harm them. However, if the record includes previous, similar allegations against your client, you could anticipate that the prosecutors will respond by arguing that the defendant is a predator who continues to use his position as a teacher to prey upon children. As a result, you will want to think of an alternative theory of the case that will be less susceptible to reversal and thus less damaging to your client.

Another advantage in preparing for all of your opponent's viable arguments is that even if not all of them are raised in the briefs, the judge or judges might raise them during oral argument (*see* "Oral Arguments," Chapter 7, pg. 63.) By anticipating counterarguments and preparing a response, you will be in better shape to respond persuasively to the judges questions. Your repeated reading of the record will also position you well for both writing a brief and oral argument. You may discover inconsistencies and omissions in the record as you become more familiar with it. The better you understand these problems, the better your ability to confront them. This step is probably the most tedious in the process, but it is important nonetheless.

* * *

A core theory brings together the law, facts, and policy into a concise statement of why your client should win. A strong core theory appeals to the judge's intellect and common sense in a way that makes him or her want to side with your client. The best briefs combine comprehensive legal research, persuasive highlighting of the most favorable facts, and an intuitive statement of why that side should win. The approach laid out in this chapter will help you formulate a strong core theory and, ultimately, a compelling brief.

CHAPTER 6

WRITING A BRIEF

I. INTRODUCTION

A. THE PURPOSE OF A BRIEF

An advocate almost always submits her case to a court in written form. In appellate courts, these documents are called briefs. A brief is a persuasive legal document designed to convince a court to rule in a party's favor. In trial courts, these documents are sometimes called memoranda of law. Despite the similarity in title, memoranda of law differ substantially from the objective legal research memoranda described in Chapter 4. To avoid confusion, this chapter uses the term "brief" to refer to a persuasive legal document, regardless of the context in which it is submitted to a court. The sample briefs in *Bell-Wesley v. O'Toole* (*see* Appendix D, pg. 121 *and* Appendix E, pg. 137) are written for submission to the Supreme Court of the State of Ames, an imaginary state supreme court. The same general principles of brief writing apply, however, to documents submitted to lower courts. A successful brief in either setting will draw upon the skills discussed in the preceding chapters, including performing legal research, synthesizing rules, developing a core theory, and structuring paragraphs of legal analysis.

A brief presents the advocate's view of her case's strongest arguments, authority, and background material in a clear and assertive manner. A strong brief is well-organized, interesting, complete, and reliable. An effective brief compels the court to rule in favor of the writer's party. The brief also serves as an aid to the court, frequently providing the foundation for a judge's decision and a resource for writing an opinion.

B. RULES OF THE COURT

Before beginning to draft your brief, be sure to review the rules of your particular court, be it moot or otherwise. Doing so prior to drafting will help avoid unnecessary shocks down the line. The rules will supply information about deadlines, page limits, format, and the sources you may consult. Follow them carefully. While these guidelines are usually included with moot court documents, you should be aware that "real-world" rules are set out both in national compilations, such as the Federal Rules of Appellate Procedure, and in local or circuit court rules.

C. OUTLINING

After you have thoroughly researched the legal issues relevant to your case and reviewed the rules of the court, the next step is to outline your brief. It can be tempting to dive straight into the writing process, but time spent outlining pays dividends when it comes to writing a well-organized, persuasive brief. At a minimum, outline your argument section. This can help you think critically about how the parts of your argument fit together, recognize areas that require more research, and structure your brief in the most persuasive manner. You will also find that the writing process goes much faster if you take the time to outline first.

D. Style

Good brief writing builds on the skills of good writing. The challenges of phrasing and structure still apply. Nonetheless, a brief is a persuasive piece of writing, and each element of your brief should work to convince the court to decide in your favor. In accomplishing this goal, a brief writer has discretion in selecting a particular writing style. Reasonable minds differ over what tone is the most persuasive. Some advocates are dispassionate, while others are more aggressive and adversarial.

No matter the tone you adopt, you should keep in mind these four basic principles:

1) Strategically select every word by analyzing its tactical value. For example, even choosing the names of the parties in the case can be significant. The overuse of "appellant" and "appellee" in a brief can be confusing to a reader who does not share your intimate understanding of the record. Instead, you should characterize the parties in a manner that will influence the reader's perception of them. For instance, you might try to evoke the reader's sympathy for a client by using a personal title while using a more formal title for an adversary. Regardless of the route you choose, you should be consistent throughout the brief.

2) Use the active voice. A forceful argument uses action verbs rather than passive forms of the verb "to be." However, keep in mind that you can downplay damaging facts and arguments by selectively and purposefully using the passive voice to minimize their impact.

3) Avoid needlessly complex language, including "legalese."

4) Avoid extended quotations. An impatient reader will skip lengthy quotations. Short quotations can be used to add variety or emphasis, but if there is no concise quotation, a paraphrase with a citation may be a better choice. Be sure to explain the relevance of the quotation; do not expect the court to figure out how it applies to your case.

E. Editing

Some writers say that there is no good writing, only good rewriting. In any case, careful editing is an essential component of a good brief, and you must budget sufficient time to edit your brief before submission. True editing, however, is more than mere proofreading. Resist the temptation to become overly attached to your writing, and think critically about how the organization of your brief could be improved. Did you follow the CRuPAC structure? Is your analysis easy to follow? At the sentence level, look out for certain word patterns that can invariably be eliminated without any loss of meaning. The following are examples of such "throat-clearing" terms: "It can be argued," "It seems that," "Cases have clearly held," "It is beyond argument that," and "One might think that." Without such phrases, prose is much clearer, stronger, and more direct. To bolster your credibility, also eliminate superfluous adverbs and adjectives where nouns and verbs will convey the same points. Be particularly careful to avoid typographical errors; careless mistakes compromise your credibility. Good form and attention to detail inspire the court's confidence in your research and analysis.

F. CONVENTION

There is no set formula for drafting a successful brief, but there are recognized conventions. This is not surprising, since writers of briefs have similar training and the common goal of persuasion. Creativity is important, particularly in crafting arguments, but it is best employed within the confines set by common practice and by the rules of your court. Accordingly, this chapter will introduce you to common brief-writing practices and the traditional components of a comprehensive appellate brief.

II. PARTS OF A BRIEF

A brief consists of several parts, each designed to convey a specific type of information. While brief writers sometimes add or omit parts depending on the particular case or court, most appellate briefs contain the following sections:

- A. Title Page;
- B. Table of Contents;
- C. Table of Authorities;
- D. Preliminary Statement;
- E. Questions Presented;
- F. Statement of Facts;
- G. Summary of the Argument;
- H. Argument;
- I. Conclusion; and
- J. Signature Block.

A. TITLE PAGE

The title page of a brief sets forth the caption, which includes the name of the court, the docket number, the names of the parties and their procedural designations (e.g., "Plaintiff-Appellant"). In most state jurisdictions and lower federal courts, the original order of the parties is maintained in the case on appeal. The Supreme Court of the United States names the appealing party first. You should also include counsels' names, formal titles (e.g., "Attorney for the Appellee"), and the date and place of the oral argument in the lower right hand corner of the page. (For examples of title pages, see the sample briefs in Appendix D, pg. 121 and Appendix E, pg. 137.)

B. TABLE OF CONTENTS

The Table of Contents should list the components of the brief, including the Table of Authorities, Preliminary Statement, Questions Presented, Statement of Facts, Summary of Argument, Argument (including complete headings and subheadings), and the Conclusion, along with the page number on which each can be found. (For examples of Tables of Contents, see the sample briefs in Appendix D, pg. 122 and Appendix E, pg. 138.)

C. Table of Authorities

Here, the writer lists all of the authorities used and notes the pages where each authority is cited in the brief. The Table of Authorities demands great technical care. Citations must be accurate and complete, and must include all of the information required by *The Bluebook* and/or the local rules of the court. All page numbers, volume numbers, underlining, parentheses, brackets, and spacing should be checked carefully before submitting a brief. (For examples of Tables of Authorities, see the sample briefs in Appendix D, pg. 123 and Appendix E, pg. 139.)

The list of citations is divided into at least three sections: "Cases," "Statutes," and "Other Sources." Arrange cases alphabetically. Sources under the "Statutes" and "Other Sources" categories should be subdivided by source type before being listed alphabetically. Under the "Statutes" section, the writer should include any constitutional provisions, court rules, or administrative regulations that are cited in the brief, expanding the section heading as needed to reflect the additional types of sources cited. Any secondary sources should be placed under the "Other Sources" category, which can be further subdivided based on the types of sources used into "Restatements," "Treatises," and "Law Review Articles."

Note that the pages of the Table of Authorities, like the Table of Contents, are traditionally numbered separately from the body of the brief, and are paginated using lowercase roman numerals. As a result, page "1" of a brief begins with the Preliminary Statement.

D. Preliminary Statement

The Preliminary Statement, sometimes called the Statement of the Case, introduces the court to the procedural posture of a case on appeal. It identifies the parties to the dispute and briefly describes the relevant procedural events leading up to the present case, including a short description of the decision and reasoning of the lower court. The preliminary statement presents the first opportunity for persuasion, so be sure to frame your statement in a compelling and succinct manner. (For examples of Preliminary Statements, see the sample briefs in Appendix D, pg. 124 and Appendix E, pg. 141.)

E. Questions Presented

The function of the Questions Presented in a brief is similar to their function in a legal research memorandum. Unlike those in a memorandum, however, the Questions Presented in a brief aim to persuade the reader to adopt a particular conclusion with a careful balance of advocacy and accuracy. A judge's initial reaction to the merit of a motion or appeal is often based upon this formulation of what the counsel considers to be vital to her case. Like the brief as a whole, the questions must be simple, interesting, complete, and reliable.

Sketching out the Questions Presented at the start of the writing process is useful because it forces the writer to frame and clarify the key issues. Some brief writers, however, prefer to save this task for last, after they have articulated their argument in detail. If you do elect to write your Questions Presented before your argument, be sure to review them afterwards to ensure you remain satisfied with them. Regardless of whether you write them first or last, you should take great care in crafting your brief's questions because the Questions Presented provide another important opportunity to present your version of the case.

1. STRUCTURE

The Questions Presented are placed at the beginning of the text in the order in which the corresponding arguments appear in the brief. Each question should be independent and require no reference to any point contained in a previous question. Although an argument may be complex, the questions should be clear and easy-to-read. Questions with many sub-clauses tend to be convoluted and should be avoided, as should wordy or overly long questions. A good rule of thumb is to keep each Question Presented under seventy-five words. However, you should not be afraid to use multiple sentences in a single Question Presented; a sentence or two of relevant factual background followed by a brief statement of the relevant law and then the question can make for a more effective and persuasive question.

2. SUBSTANCE

The questions should suggest the answers the writer wants the court to reach. Put another way, a reader should always be able to tell which side wrote a brief simply by reading the Questions Presented. An effective Question Presented gently suggests that the court can reasonably rule in only one way—in the writer's favor. Be careful, however, not to irritate the court with overly biased questions that suggest by their stridency the inevitable counter-argument. To achieve this balance, questions should mesh important facts with the law that the writer wants the court to apply. It may be tempting to craft lofty, abstract questions of law, but you should resist the temptation and remember that fact-filled questions will help you impart some of the flavor of your argument to the reader from the very start.

Be careful in your questions not to assume the issue in dispute. For example, the question "Does an unreasonable search violate the Fourth Amendment?" assumes that the search in question was unreasonable. This question is poorly crafted, because the real issue is whether the particular search in the case was an unreasonable search. There is no question that if the search were unreasonable, it would violate the Fourth Amendment.

Finally, the Questions Presented should be answerable by either a "yes" or a "no." For purpose of symmetry, try to frame all of the questions in a brief so that they are answered the same way—either all "yes" or all "no"—in support of your position.

3. SAMPLE QUESTIONS

Different advocates arguing *Bell-Wesley v. O'Toole* might draft the following Questions Presented:

1. Is a doctor who negligently performs a vasectomy liable for the costs of raising a child when the husband subsequently impregnates his wife and they have an unplanned baby?

2. Where a couple, after having several congenitally deformed children who died soon after birth, has a child conceived after an unsuccessfully performed vasectomy, and refused to abort, or give the child up for adoption, should the doctor who performed the vasectomy be held

liable for all the costs of raising that child when the couple could well afford to have the child, and benefited from the doctor's negligence by receiving the healthy child that they had always wanted?

3. O'Toole negligently performed a vasectomy and follow-up testing on Scott Bell-Wesley. As a result of O'Toole's negligence, the Bell-Wesleys unexpectedly conceived and gave birth to a son, incurring the costs of his delivery and upbringing. Under fundamental tort law principles, individuals are liable for all injuries flowing naturally and foreseeably from their negligence. Should O'Toole be held liable for the full results of his negligence, including the extensive costs associated with raising a child?

The most effective question is the third one. It clearly suggests the answer the litigant wants the court to reach: "yes." It incorporates key facts of the case, such as the negligent sterilization, and uses phrases like "full results of his negligence" and "extensive costs" to set the tone for the subsequent argument. It also clearly identifies the core legal issues.

By contrast, the first question is not persuasive enough. The reader cannot tell which side the author represents. The use of "negligently" suggests she represents the couple, but the phrase "unplanned baby" is not favorable to the couple and the author does not lead the reader to any answer. Additionally, few facts are incorporated into the question. While a brief writer should strive for concise Questions Presented, this question is incomplete.

Complicated and difficult to follow, Question 2 errs in the other direction. Although it is clear the writer represents the doctor, the author uses too many clauses and is likely to lose rather than persuade her reader. While certain slanted phrases, like "the healthy child that they had always wanted" show promise, they are lost in the complexity of an unwieldy question.

A good brief should avoid overly simplistic questions, like Question 1, and confusing questions, like Question 2. Instead, seek a middle ground, as in Question 3. (For examples of effective Questions Presented, see the sample briefs in *Bell-Wesley v. O'Toole* in Appendix D, pg. 124 and Appendix E, pg. 141.)

F. STATEMENT OF FACTS

The Statement of Facts presents your view of what happened in the "real world" to bring this case into court. For example, each side in *Bell-Wesley v. O'Toole* informs the court about the couple's decision that Scott would have a vasectomy:

> **Sample Statement of Facts excerpts:**
>
> The attorney for the Bell-Wesleys writes:
>
> The Bell-Wesleys made a conscious decision to forego having children. R. at 1. They made this difficult decision after they previously had given birth to three children, all of whom tragically died within six months of birth due to a genetic congenital disorder. Id. Their doctor, Defendant-Appellee Stephen O'Toole, advised the Bell-Wesleys that there was a seventy-five percent chance that any future child they conceived would suffer from the same lethal congenital disorder. Id. Based on O'Toole's advice and their fear of bringing another ill child into the world, the Bell-Wesleys chose to

> remain childless. R. at 1, 11. They did not adopt. See id. Instead, they devoted their lives to each other and to their careers. See R. at 3, 9.

(*See* Appendix D, pg. 125.)

In contrast, the attorney for Dr. O'Toole writes:

> On three occasions before the January 2011 birth of their son, the Bell-Wesleys attempted to start a family. R. at 1. Each time, however, Ms. Bell-Wesley gave birth to a sick infant that died within six months due to a fatal congenital abnormality. R. at 1. Dr. O'Toole accurately informed the Bell-Wesleys that there was a seventy-five percent chance that any child they conceived would suffer from the same abnormality. R. at 1. For the sole purpose of avoiding the conception of another sick child, the Bell-Wesleys decided to have Mr. Bell-Wesley sterilized. R. at 7.

(*See* Appendix E, pg. 141.)

Note that both sides describe the same essential facts but use very different language. The Bell-Wesleys stress the "conscious decision to forego having children," while Dr. O'Toole emphasizes that the "sole purpose" of the decision was to avoid the "conception of another sick child." The authors cite the Record in the case throughout.

The Statement of Facts in a brief, unlike the Statement of Facts in a legal memorandum, should be persuasive rather than objective. (For a discussion of the Statement of Facts in a legal memorandum, see Chapter 4, pg. 31.) Note that persuasive does not mean false or distorted. While the Statement of Facts in each sample brief tells the story from a different perspective, neither writer crosses the line into drawing unsupported conclusions, exaggerating, or misleading the court.

Both sides must present a complete and reliable, yet easy-to-understand and interesting, version of the facts of the case. To some judges, a fair yet persuasive Statement of Facts can be more dispositive than a carefully crafted Argument. After reading your Statement of Facts, the judge should want to interpret the law in your favor.

1. CHOOSING THE FACTS

Separate the relevant facts from the irrelevant ones in the record. Be careful, however, not to omit the most relevant facts supporting your opponent's position. A failure to disclose important, albeit unfavorable, facts is likely to impair your credibility with the court. Still, a good Statement of the Facts will do more than just summarize the record; it will shape the relevant facts into a narrative that interests the reader and favors the author's position.

Also make sure that your Statement of Facts includes every fact mentioned in your Argument; there should be no factual surprises buried in your Argument. To this end, make sure to reread your Statement of Facts after you have finished writing your Argument section to be sure that all necessary facts are included. While a seemingly obvious point, it is easy to recognize the importance of a particular fact while crafting your Argument but then forget to include it in the Statement of Facts once the Argument is finished.

2. USING THE RECORD

Use only the facts found in the record or facts of general knowledge, which are subject to "judicial notice." You can use admissions by the other side as positive proof of a fact considered material. Regardless of the source, be sure to support your factual assertions with proper citations.

The creativity you demonstrate in presenting a persuasive fact must not extend to fabricating or exaggerating information. A judge will not let a fabricated "fact" slide by as a clever inference. All assumptions of fact must be firmly grounded in the record. Certain undeniable assertions, however, such as the fact that apples do not fall up, can be used without appearing in the record. Other information, like the conclusions of relevant sociological studies, can be used even though they are not part of the record as long as proper authority is cited.

Holes in the record can also prove useful in a brief. You can successfully use "negative facts" to buttress your position. Negative facts are facts that the other side can neither establish nor disprove, because they do not exist in the record. For example, the *Bell-Wesley v. O'Toole* record is silent on the issue of whether Scott and Rebecca ever considered adopting a child after learning that there was a high likelihood that any child they conceived would suffer a congenital birth defect. Nonetheless, in the appellants' brief, the author uses this negative fact to support a favorable inference:

> Based on O'Toole's advice and their fear of bringing another ill child into the world, the Bell-Wesleys chose to remain childless. R. at 1, 11. They did not adopt. See id. Instead, they devoted their lives to each other and to their careers. See R. at 3, 9.

(*See* Appendix D, pg. 125.) Do not be afraid to make effective use of holes in the record that can help shape a favorable presentation of the facts of the case.

3. ORGANIZING THE FACTS

The organization of the facts is critical because how the judge views the facts will undoubtedly influence how she views the case. Every word in the Statement of Facts should be geared toward making the brief a better instrument of persuasion and a more complete and reliable resource. A chronological, carefully constructed narrative is often the most persuasive structure for telling the story of your case. Alternatively, you can try starting with the conflict or injury and later describing what preceded it. With either approach, remember these points:

- Use labels that appropriately characterize the parties.
- Use words with effective connotations for your argument.
- Never assume the reader has any prior knowledge of the case. Introduce the parties and avoid abbreviations with which the court may not be familiar.

4. HANDLING ADVERSE FACTS

Glaring omissions of adverse facts central to the other side's case will decrease your credibility with the court and lessen the persuasive power of your brief. More strategically, omitting adverse facts also costs you the opportunity to mitigate the damage those facts can cause. Carefully disclosing adverse facts in the Statement of Facts thus serves the dual purpose of preserving your credibility with the court and allowing you to present otherwise damaging facts in the best possible light.

Downplay unfavorable facts by being strategic about how you present them. Consider using the passive voice to help dilute their force. You can also place damaging material in subordinate clauses of longer sentences or in the middle of a paragraph to minimize its impact. Once a harmful fact is mentioned, there is no need to emphasize it. For example, while an appellant needs to disclose that there was an adverse judgment below, she need not disclose that the district judge rejected each and every contention. Rest assured that the appellee will mention that. For another example, in *Bell-Wesley v. O'Toole*, the doctor's attorney minimized his client's negligence by saying Dr. O'Toole "performed a vasectomy" and "mistakenly informed" Mr. Bell-Wesley that he was sterile. (*See* Appendix E, pg. 142.) On the other hand, the Bell-Wesleys' attorney used language like "botched the procedure" and "then compounded his surgical error" to characterize the same acts in a light favorable to his clients. (*See* Appendix D, pg. 125.)

5. Separating Fact from Argument

Paint a persuasive factual picture, but guard against the temptation to cross the boundary into argument. The facts are used to support conclusions, but they must not be expressed as conclusions. For example, a Statement of Facts should not contain conclusions of law such as "the defendant acted knowingly and recklessly." Instead, explain what the defendant did, allowing the court to reach its own conclusion that the defendant acted in that manner. The court should be left to draw the appropriate legal conclusion once you have provided the factual foundation. One exception to this rule—as demonstrated in the sample briefs—is that you may report the conclusions of law of the lower court(s) in a Statement of Facts for an appellate brief. (*See, e.g.*, Appendix D, pg. 125 and Appendix E, pg. 141.)

G. Summary of the Argument

A one- or two-paragraph road map outlining the party's essential arguments is incredibly useful, particularly in complex cases. A good Summary of the Argument is clear and concise and contains few citations. You should also use the section to acquaint the reader with your core theory of the case. For example, the attorney for the Bell-Wesleys used her Summary of the Argument to stress her view that Dr. O'Toole's negligence should not be excused simply because one of the products of his negligence was a child. (*See* Appendix D, pg. 127.) Rules governing the location of the Summary of the Argument vary by jurisdiction, so be sure to check your court's rules.

H. Argument

The argument section comprises the majority of the brief. After considering legal precedent, policy, and the facts of the case, choose the strongest arguments to include in your brief. Discard weaker or less clear arguments because including them will dilute the force of your main points. Buttress your arguments with authority, and strive to anticipate, preempt, or rebut your opponent's core arguments and to distinguish opposing cases.

1. Argument Headings

Each argument begins with a complete sentence called an "argument heading." The heading should be a concise summary of the argument. The heading identifies the specific portion of the argument to be advanced in that section of the brief, and it is particularly important given the heavy caseloads many judges face. To create an effective heading, imagine that a judge only has a few minutes to scan through your brief and that she focuses on your headings alone. She should be able to understand and follow the general progress of your argument if your headings are crafted properly.

The argument headings should state affirmatively the resolution of the issues raised in the Questions Presented. An effective argument heading will identify the applicable law, the way in which the law applies to the facts of the case at hand, and the conclusion that follows from that application. A good rule of thumb is that if you could copy your heading into another brief and it would still fit, you have not sufficiently tailored your heading to the facts of your case. Of course, not every relevant legal or factual issue can fit in a heading, and headings should not be so long as to be difficult to read and understand. Argument headings are conventionally identified by roman numerals and comprised of bolded, single spaced, capital letters.

2. Subheadings

Subheadings may be used effectively to partition arguments, especially complex ones. When an argument is relatively simple, however, subheadings may interrupt the flow of the argument. Subheadings are identified by capital letters, while the text of the subheading itself typically uses lower case letters and is bolded.

> **Example of an argument heading and subheadings:**
> **I. THIS COURT SHOULD NOT AWARD THE APPELLANTS DAMAGES FOR THE COSTS OF RAISING THEIR NORMAL, HEALTHY SON TO MAJORITY**
>
> **A. Frank's Birth Did Not Injure the Appellants Because Giving Birth to a Healthy Child Cannot be an "Injury"**
>
> **B. Even if the Birth of Appellants' Son Constitutes an "Injury," Frank's Birth Did Not Cause a Compensable Economic Injury to the Bell-Wesleys Because They Sought Sterilization for Purely Non-Economic Reasons**

(Appendix E, pg. 138.)

The sample argument heading above identifies the legal issue of damages and the author's position. The subheadings describe how the law relates to the specific facts of the case: *because* the Bell-Wesleys sought sterilization for non-economic reasons, they suffered no legally cognizable injury. Furthermore, the subheadings neatly break the main argument down into its legal and policy components. Finally, the argument heading and subheadings are not bolstered by unnecessary adverbs or adjectives.

Depending on the complexity of a case's legal arguments, a brief may also incorporate additional layers of subheadings, typically marked by Arabic numerals. You should be careful not to make a brief's outline overly complex, but another layer of subheadings is useful if a particular subheading can be cleanly divided into substantial, independent sections. A judge should be able to read through the headings and subheadings of a brief and have a complete picture of the arguments.

3. STANDARD OF REVIEW

An appellate brief should set forth the appropriate standard of review explicitly in the Argument section of the brief. The standard of review dictates how an appeals court must treat the findings of a lower court and guides the court's analysis. You should provide the Standard of Review for each Question Presented. Generally, an appeals court must defer to a trial court's findings of fact, disturbing them only if they are "clearly erroneous." However, an appeals court typically may make its own determinations on the law regardless of the trial court decision. This is called "de novo" review.

The distinction between issues of fact and law is not always readily apparent, so consider your case carefully and be sure to research the standard of review for the particular cause of action involved. A case from the appropriate jurisdiction will usually clarify the standard of review. For example, in some contract cases, an appellate judge may make new findings on the interpretation of a contract term, but she should defer to the trial judge's assessment of oral testimony.

If the parties disagree about the appropriate standard of review, then the "correct" standard of review should be argued rather than merely asserted. Logistically, the standard of review may be included in the first paragraph of the first argument. Alternatively, it may be placed in a separate section between the Statement of Facts and the Argument. In some instances, you will want to present the standard of review in an argument subheading. The prominence of the standard of review in a brief will depend on how favorable it is to your side and whether it is a point of contention.

If the standard of review is favorable, you should use it to frame your arguments throughout the brief. For example, you may frame the Questions Presented or Argument headings in light of the standard of review. Similarly, an attorney for the appellee who won in the trial court will often stress the "clearly erroneous" standard. The appellant, however, will emphasize that no deference should be given to the trial court's interpretation of the law.

> **Discussing the standard of review:**
> The Bell-Wesleys' brief:
> Whether the Bell-Wesley family can recover the full cost of raising a healthy child as an element of damages in a wrongful pregnancy action is a question of law and thus reviewed *de novo*. See Lovelace Med. Ctr. v. Mendez, 805 P.2d 603, 614 (N.M. 1991).
>
> (*See* Appendix D, pg. 128.)

In the example above, the attorney for the appellants, the Bell-Wesleys, stresses that the appellate court need not follow the trial court's refusal to recognize a cause of action for wrongful birth. In contrast, the attorney for Dr. O'Toole downplays the standard of review for legal findings by keeping the discussion succinct.

4. Form of the Argument

The argument should follow the CRuPAC method discussed in Chapter 1. You should choose what legal issues to discuss so that they proceed in a logical order and mirror the structure that you have laid out elsewhere in your brief in your Questions Presented and Summary of the Argument.

5. Substance of the Argument

The argument musters facts and law to persuade the court to rule in your side's favor. Do not devote long sections of the brief, for example, to the historical evolution of a current legal standard. This style is simply not persuasive to a court which must apply principles of law to the particular facts of the case. A skillful brief writer will attempt to incorporate direct references to the relevant facts of the case into every paragraph of the argument.

Because unsupported assertions are not persuasive, you must provide citations to the cases and other authorities that give the court the tools to reach a particular decision. When properly used, authorities aid in convincing the reader to adopt the propositions asserted. The authorities with the greatest relevance (those most "on point") and the greatest weight should be cited. Cases with similar facts and issues are usually the most relevant, and decisions that bind your court have the greatest weight. (For more on the use of authorities, see Chapter 2, pg. 12.) Citing a variety of jurisdictions, however, may be useful to show that courts widely accept a proposition. Uncontested propositions of law, such as the definition of negligence, rarely require more than one authority in a citation.

While major cases should be discussed at appropriate length, others can be effectively summarized by using parentheticals. In some instances, the best way to use a case is to paraphrase the principle it stands for and follow that with a citation. However, an unelaborated or "bare" cite, giving only the case name and the reporter, will not often help the court. Parentheticals, abstracting the holding of the case or quoting critical language, aid the reader by explaining the relevance, similarity, or difference of the cited case to the case at hand.

> **Example of an explanatory parenthetical:**
>
> The general rule in tort cases is that "a person has an obligation to exercise reasonable care so as to not cause foreseeable harm to another." Marciniak v. Lundborg, 450 N.W.2d 243, 245 (Wis. 1989) (citation omitted) (holding that costs of raising child to majority may be recovered by parents as damages for negligently performed sterilization procedure).
>
> (*See* Appendix D, pg. 128)

While parentheticals can be useful, do not overuse them. Your most important cases will often need more extensive treatment than a parenthetical provides. An advocate might include a paragraph explaining how the legal principle in an opinion governs the issue before the court, or why it must be distinguished. In either situation, the relevant facts from the case before the court should be emphasized for their similarities or differences to the facts of the opinion cited.

For the sake of reliability and completeness, you should also cite important cases standing *against* the propositions advanced in your brief. The ethical rules of most jurisdictions require citation of controlling contrary authority. However, you can lessen the effect of contrary authority in two ways: 1) by distinguishing your case based on the facts or the rationale, or 2) by undermining the rationale of the contrary authority. The first method allows you to argue that the contrary authority should not be controlling in your case because the facts are too dissimilar or because the rationale that motivated the court's decision in that instance does not apply to your case.

The second method, undermining rather than distinguishing a contrary authority, requires a more direct attack on the contrary court's reasoning and should be used with care. When cited as adverse to the proposition raised, a contrary authority should be signaled with *"but see."* Citation of contrary authority shows thoroughness, enhancing your credibility with the court. It also negates the damage done by the adverse cases because it gives you the opportunity to shape the way the court interprets the contrary authority.

Once you have discussed the legal precedent that supports your position and dealt with any binding, contrary authorities, be sure to survey the case law for any relevant policy arguments. Roughly speaking, any argument that the outcome benefits the public interest falls into this category. Some brief writers place public policy arguments under separate headings. Often, however, they appear in a separate paragraph under a particular argument heading. For example, the attorney for Dr. O'Toole makes a public policy argument about the effect of awarding full damages. According to the writer, deciding in Dr. O'Toole's favor furthers the public policy against unreasonable liability for physicians. (*See* Appendix E, pg. 146.) When analyzing and interpreting precedents, try to determine what policy rationales underlie them and the implications of those rationales for your case.

Finally, an advocate who urges a change or modification of the law as it has developed in cases should include references to scholars or other authorities that have also argued for such a change. This may make the court more "comfortable" with departing from precedent or navigating uncharted territory. (For examples of uses of law review articles, see the sample briefs in Appendix D, pg. 130 and Appendix E, pg. 144.)

6. Preemption and Rebuttal of Arguments

A good appellant brief should anticipate the appellee's best counterarguments and respond to them, explaining why those arguments ultimately fail. Similarly, effective appellee briefs must address the appellant's best arguments. Avoiding or concealing the difficult points in your argument may leave their resolution to the court without the benefit of your guidance. Instead, try to show the logical deficiencies of your opponent's argument, demonstrate how the facts fail to support their legal conclusion, or point out the unfortunate consequences that would flow from a decision for the other side.

Regardless, the tone of each brief must remain affirmative and not convey a defensive posture. Blanket statements characterizing the other side as wrong are useless and may detract from your credibility. When responding to counterarguments, however, be careful not to simply summarize the other side's arguments. This wastes space and puts the writer in a purely defensive position. You should counter the arguments effectively and succinctly, and watch that you do not cross the line into making your opponent's arguments for him.

A respondent or appellee should use any opportunity to review the brief of the moving party, or appellant, before she files her own brief. Because the time between filings is usually short, the respondent must not wait until she has received the appellant's brief before she begins researching and preparing her arguments. Once she has the appellant's brief, however, the respondent should use it to highlight the weaknesses of the moving party's arguments. Still, a point-by-point refutation is rarely the ideal format for a respondent's brief. Independent arguments are stronger and more persuasive.

7. Arguing in the Alternative

For some legal arguments there are "fall-back" positions. If the court fails to agree with one side's main position, the court can turn to the advocate's alternative argument. For example, the Bell-Wesleys' attorney argues that based on the law and facts, the Bell-Wesleys should receive full child-rearing damages. In the alternative, she argues that if the court does not award full child-rearing damages, the court should award full recovery offset by the value of the emotional benefits the Bell-Wesleys receive from Frank. (*See* Appendix D, pg. 133.)

Arguing in the alternative should never force you to compromise your core theory. If an alternative argument contradicts your core theory, you might choose to omit it from the brief and reserve it for oral argument. If the judges are not receptive to your main argument, then you may raise the alternative one.

I. Conclusion

The brief ends with a section entitled, "Conclusion," which clearly states the remedy or relief sought. A summary is usually *unhelpful* here. Because it is difficult to determine which components of an argument a court will find persuasive, emphasizing one or the other in summary may undermine the persuasive effect of the winning argument. Also, page limits may require you to leave out details.

What you should always do in a Conclusion is tell the court what you want it to do—to reverse or affirm the lower court's judgment in an appeals case, or to hold a certain way in a district court case. Always remember that your job as an advocate is to achieve a certain outcome for your client. Make sure that you clearly articulate at the end of your brief what you want that outcome to be.

J. Signature Block

Different courts have different requirements for the Signature Block, but typically you can expect to include a closing line (e.g., "Respectfully submitted"), the typed names of the brief's authors, their addresses, their signatures, and the date of submission.

III. SAMPLE BRIEFS: *BELL-WESLEY V. O'TOOLE*

Sample briefs for the appellants and appellee in the case of *Bell-Wesley v. O'Toole* appear in Appendix D and Appendix E, respectively.

As you know from reading the sample Record in Appendix C, this case involves a wrongful pregnancy action. On appeal, the legal issue is whether or not the Bell-Wesleys should receive damages for the costs of raising their son Frank, who was born after Dr. O'Toole negligently performed a vasectomy and sperm count.

The brief for Dr. O'Toole argues that the Bell-Wesleys should not receive any child-rearing costs. It cites supportive legal authority, stressing that the reason the Bell-Wesleys obtained sterilization, to avoid the birth of another sick baby, means they cannot recover for any costs beyond the prenatal period. It also reviews public policy reasons for this position.

The attorney for Dr. O'Toole recognizes that the Bell-Wesleys will argue that they should receive full costs, but that the court could still apply the equitable "benefit rule" to offset damages by the amount of the benefit the Bell-Wesleys receive from having their son Frank. Therefore, the brief for Dr. O'Toole contests that the "benefit rule" is inapplicable when the intangible benefits of a child are involved. Nonetheless, the writer maintains that even if the court adopts the "benefit rule," it should still find that the benefit to the Bell-Wesleys outweighs the costs.

The brief for the Bell-Wesleys argues that they should receive all damages flowing naturally from the negligence of Dr. O'Toole. Their side has far less legal authority upon which to rely, but they have many convincing policy arguments. The Bell-Wesleys also argue in the alternative that if the judge refuses to award full damages because of the benefit bestowed on them through the birth of a healthy child, the judge should apply the offset rule (providing them with full recovery less the amount of the benefit they derive from the child).

Take a moment now to read through both briefs to get a better idea of what the tips and tools presented in this Chapter look like in practice.

CHAPTER 7

ORAL ARGUMENTS

The oral argument is the culmination of your efforts as an advocate. Although only used sparingly in trial courts (e.g. summary judgment motions), oral argument plays an important role in appellate advocacy and has become an historic part of American advocacy. In the early years of the Supreme Court, arguments lasted for hours, if not days. Although increased caseloads have caused modern courts to reduce the availability and length of arguments, oral argument still presents a valuable opportunity to convince the court of the merits of your case and to dispel any doubts particular judges may have after reading the briefs.

Presenting an effective oral argument is different from brief writing in a number of ways. First, it is an interactive effort requiring spontaneous responses to the judges' questions. Second, it takes place under strict time limits, so you must prioritize arguments even more radically than in the brief. Finally, the effectiveness of oral argument depends in large part on the attorney's physical presence and speaking style. Despite these differences, the oral argument is a logical extension of the brief, building on its foundations. If you are prepared to defend your core theory and are familiar with the supporting case law and the record, you will be able to answer the judges' questions confidently. As in brief writing, diverse styles and approaches may be equally successful. There is no one right way to frame an oral argument. There are, however, some basics to master and tips to help you succeed. Accordingly, in this Chapter you will find information on how to prepare for oral arguments, how to organize your argument, how to respond to questions, and how to present yourself effectively.

In appellate litigation, our model for this chapter, the structure of an oral argument is simple and direct. The appellant (or "petitioner") rises first to introduce the case and to explain why the court should reverse the lower tribunal's decision. The appellee (or "respondent") then argues her side of the case, defending the lower court's decision. Finally, the appellant may choose to rebut her opponent's assertions. Throughout the argument, the judges are likely to interrupt counsels' presentations with questions. Attention to the judges' concerns and creative responses to any hypothetical situations they may pose are often the most important features of a good oral argument.

I. PREPARING FOR ORAL ARGUMENT

In preparing for oral argument you should focus on both substance and style. Carefully study the record, relevant authorities, and arguments that will enable you to defend your brief and to answer the judges' questions. Practice delivering your argument so that you become comfortable with public speaking and the phrasing of your case. This practice will also help ensure that you are not distracted or trapped by questions, that you can transition effectively between different parts of your argument, and that you emphasize your key points. At the same time, you should avoid rote memorization and canned, mechanical responses. A good oralist is both prepared and flexible, inventing appropriate responses on the spot when necessary and being sensitive to the personalities and concerns of the judges.

Now that you know some of the qualities of an excellent oralist, you may wonder where to begin your own preparation. The following is a step-by-step outline of basic techniques to help you prepare your oral argument.

A. STUDY THE RECORD AND AUTHORITIES

Success in oral argument requires detailed knowledge of the record. It is important to understand, and have an identifiable point of view on, the events giving rise to the cause of action and the facts and issues discussed in the lower court's opinion. The court is more likely to trust other aspects of your argument if you have a solid command of the record, whereas an incomplete knowledge of the record will only hurt your credibility in the eyes of the judges.

Likewise, studying the cases included in both sides' briefs is a vital step in your argument preparation. Judges often use the oral arguments to determine which cases should guide their decision and whether the parties' arguments based on precedent are consistent. You should prepare to analogize your case to helpful precedents and distinguish it from harmful ones. Writing short case abstracts and indexing the record is both a helpful study process and can enable easy referencing during the argument. However, these notes should not become a crutch. An advocate who can discuss the cases and facts without frequently referring to notes will have a more natural dialogue with the judge, and thus, may be more successful.

In addition to considering the authorities cited in both briefs, you may also want to consider authorities that were not raised previously. Depending on the rules of the court (some courts restrict the use of cases not cited in the briefs), new authorities that were not presented in your brief sometimes may be raised orally before the court. You may use this opportunity to correct what the judges perceive as ambiguities or flaws in the original brief.

B. ANALYZE THE ARGUMENTS

Not every aspect of your brief can make it into your oral argument. You will need to make strategic choices as to which arguments are most important and amenable to oral presentation. Choosing effective arguments for oral presentation often means separating the wheat from the chaff of an argument. Before you do so, try to break down the arguments presented in both parties' briefs. A fresh look at the arguments will give you a complete background against which to make strategic and tactical choices concerning both substance and style. Although there may be many reasons to find for your client, your job is to emphasize what you see as the most important reasons, the most compelling reasons, or those reasons that may have the most influence on the court. The following guidelines can aid you in selecting and refining arguments.

1. USE YOUR CORE THEORY

The demands of oral argument illustrate the importance of having a pithy, convincing core theory—a one or two sentence explanation of the essence of a party's position. (For a review of core theory, see Chapter 5.) Both a good brief and a good oral argument will stress a central theme, approaching that theme from different angles based on the relevant facts, law, and policy. Yet in oral argument, you should be prepared to express your core theory even more simply and memorably than in your brief. Accordingly, when organizing your argument, keep in mind the relationship between each assertion and your core theory. Try to weave your points together with your core theory to craft a cohesive argument that the judges will remember. With your core theory as your guide, you should be able to place your answers to the judges' questions in context and to rebut your opponent's arguments. To this end, know that you are not shackled to your brief during oral argument and that you are free to focus on the points you choose. Thus, while you may have spent a relatively small portion of your brief addressing public policy concerns, you are free to emphasize those concerns in your argument if you feel it will persuade the judges and fit with your theory of the case.

2. REVIEW AND PRIORITIZE SPECIFIC ARGUMENTS

Working from the briefs, you should outline and review the specific arguments made by both parties. This may require some new thought about which arguments are the most convincing or the most controversial. The limited time frame of oral argument means that not all of a party's arguments will be developed fully. Keeping in mind the desired results of the litigation, rank arguments in terms of their importance in achieving those results. There is no single method for prioritizing. Some factors to weigh include: 1) whether a written argument is simple enough to make orally; 2) what policy considerations may move a judge to rule favorably; 3) what argument the judges are likely to want clarified; 4) what argument is most closely related to the facts; and 5) whether an argument follows or goes against current trends in the law.

Arguing for a change in the law may be a strong choice in some situations, but often it meets with greater resistance from the court and will require more justification than an argument for the status quo. Thus, you should typically avoid characterizing your legal position as something novel or unique. Rather, you should emphasize how—under your theory of the case—precedent and reason dictate a verdict in favor of your client. To do so, you must know exactly what the lower court did and exactly what you seek to have affirmed or reversed.

Finally, when prioritizing your arguments, be sure to consider what opposing counsel will likely focus on during oral arguments. This will help you identify the key issues on which the case might turn, allowing you to anticipate lines of questioning from the judges. It will also help you to identify potential weaknesses in your own arguments that you will need to explain under tight time constraints. While you will want to use the majority of your argument time to present your own case affirmatively, you may also choose to use a few moments to explain why a particular counterargument is incorrect or otherwise not persuasive.

C. STRATEGY AND STYLE

The oral argument should be a conversation with the judges in which you discuss your view of how the case should be resolved and address any doubts the judges have about your interpretation of the facts and the law.

While you absolutely should conduct yourself as a zealous advocate for your client, a conversational demeanor in oral arguments will serve you well. In other words, yelling, podium-pounding, and sarcastic responses make for great television but terrible oral arguments. Instead, you will want to let the strength of your position shine through your arguments to the court and your answers to the judges' questions. By providing believable answers that eliminate their doubts, you will persuade them to decide in favor of your client. The judges' questions may not be predictable, but in the overwhelming majority of cases, they are not designed to trick you. If you are well-prepared and a good listener, you will have no trouble answering any questions they may raise.

A good oral argument is neither an overly rehearsed monologue, nor is it an oral recitation of the brief. The argument should be lively, vivid, and occasionally improvised. If need be, use a clever illustration to make a point clear. Pick up on the judges' metaphors and hypothetical situations, and suggest your own. Often, nothing is more persuasive than using an example that the judges can picture vividly in their minds, because that image is likely to be remembered long after your presentation.

Another key preparation strategy is to think about the institutional factors that might influence a judge's attitudes. What arguments are likely to appeal to a particular judge based on ideological preferences? Will the bench be "hot," where the judges ask many questions, or "cold," where the judges rarely intervene? Are the judges likely to have read your brief before your argument? Any predictions as to these factors will be just that—predictions—but often, devoting some thought to these factors will better prepare you for the nature of your conversation with the panel.

Similarly, you should know the different advantages of representing the appellant or the appellee. The appellant speaks first and has the opportunity to raise particular issues and to set the tone of the argument. The appellee, on the other hand, can tailor her argument to concerns of the court as demonstrated in questions to the appellant. The opportunity for rebuttal gives the appellant the coveted last word, but in another sense, the appellee has the upper hand since the appellant seeks to overturn a lower court judgment already entered against her. Both parties should also be aware of the applicable standard of review and, at the very least, be ready to advise the court about that standard. At best, you can use the standard of review advantageously in making an argument either to respect or to reverse the district court's judgment.

D. Practice, Practice, Practice

To best prepare yourself for oral arguments, you should rehearse in the most realistic way possible. Practice your delivery out loud and experiment with different emphases and timing. If you have the opportunity, try recording your performance—reviewing a recorded performance will expose weaknesses in your delivery like awkward phrases, hesitations, wordiness, distracting movements, or mumbling. You should also recruit at least one practice questioner to act as a judge and force you to practice responding to questions on the spot. In addition to making your delivery stronger, these practice techniques also lead to substantive improvements because flaws in your argument become clearer when stated out loud and questioned. Finally, rehearsing this new skill will build your confidence, which will in turn make you a more effective oralist.

II. ORGANIZING THE ORAL ARGUMENT

A. THE BASIC STRUCTURE OF ORAL ARGUMENT

There are many ways to build an effective argument, and an appellee's argument in particular may differ from the traditional model we describe below as a matter of strategy. However, most oral presentations do conform, at least roughly, to this framework. What would a judge like to know first about the case? What manner of presentation would immediately inform the judge of the central issue? What is an interesting, logical, respectful, and positive approach? The oral argument model we discuss here is a common-sense way of answering these questions.

1. THE OPENING STATEMENT

The opening statement introduces you as counsel and describes the nature of the case. You should introduce yourself in a formal and simple way by giving your name and the names of your clients. For example:

> May it please the court, my name is Jane Harvey. I represent the appellants, Rebecca and Scott Bell-Wesley.

In moot court exercises with teams of speakers, the first speaker should introduce both herself and her teammate. The second speaker will repeat her own name before launching into her half of the argument.

In addition, the first speaker should outline for the court the issues that each of the advocates will develop. A proper introduction of the issues should combine essential facts and legal analysis to describe the case in a nutshell, and it should enable the judges to focus on specific issues presented. The introduction should highlight the core theory and give the court enough information to follow the arguments. Consider the following sample introduction, given on behalf of the Bell-Wesleys:

> This case is here on appeal from the Court of Appeals for the State of Ames. The Bell-Wesleys urge this Court to overturn the lower court's ruling that child-rearing costs are not recoverable in a wrongful pregnancy action.
>
> I will argue that the fundamental principles of tort law dictate that child-rearing damages are recoverable to the same extent as any other reasonably foreseeable consequence of standard medical malpractice. My co-counsel, Yvonne Smith, will argue that even if this Court will not award full damages, it should compensate the Bell-Wesleys for the extensive costs of raising a child, offset by the benefit of having the child.

From this statement, the court knows at the outset what the questions are and will be able to listen to the facts and arguments with some appreciation of their relevance.

By comparison, an opening that launches into a contorted description of procedural history or immediately begins reciting facts will not give the court adequate background. Confusing openings like these should be avoided:

> **Introductions to avoid:**
>
> *The overly procedural introduction*: This case comes here on appeal of a judgment entered by the Superior Court for the State of Ames. The Superior Court rejected Plaintiff's claim for damages, and the Court of Appeals also declined to award the requested damages. The Plaintiffs then petitioned this Court, which granted certiorari to determine whether the Bell-Wesleys can recover the costs of raising their son.
>
> *The overly factual introduction*: The Plaintiffs here seek damages in the form of full child-rearing costs because Dr. O'Toole performed a negligent vasectomy on Mr. Bell-Wesley on October 16, 2005, when he failed to sever the tubes of Mr. Bell-Wesley's vas deferens properly, leaving him capable of fathering another child. Dr. O'Toole then negligently conducted a sperm count, incorrectly informing Mr. Bell-Wesley that he was sterile. As a result of Dr. Toole's negligence, the Bell-Wesleys gave birth to a son, Frank, on January 4, 2008.

As these contrasting examples demonstrate, a clear presentation is crucial. You should not plunge into facts or procedural history without a true introduction.

2. ROADMAP OF LEGAL ARGUMENTS

After introducing yourself and the case, you should give the court a concise outline of the legal arguments you will develop to support your position. The appellant in *Bell-Wesley v. O'Toole,* speaking on the first issue (recovering full damages), might present her outline in the following manner:

> There are two bases for the Bell-Wesleys' claim for child rearing damages. First, Dr. O'Toole's behavior contains all the elements necessary to prove medical malpractice such that fundamental tort law principles require full and fair compensation for the Bell-Wesleys. Second, awarding compensation to the Bell-Wesleys would support public policies favoring family planning, self-determination, and trust between doctor and patient.

This summary outline gives the judges a pattern in which to fit later arguments, indicates the order in which matters will be discussed, and enables the court to defer its questions until the appropriate time. Moreover, announcing the arguments at the beginning of a presentation—albeit in abbreviated form—will at least communicate that these particular arguments are important, even if lengthy questioning on an early point precludes discussing all of the topics prepared for discussion.

3. STATEMENT OF FACTS

The parties' briefs provide the relevant facts of the case. Accordingly, the oral statement of the facts should be relatively concise. Absent a particular strategic rationale, i.e. the facts are extremely important or particularly strong, any lengthy exposition of the facts wastes valuable time and raises the risk of getting bogged down in factual minutiae. Therefore, rather than providing an exhaustive chronology, the most important function of the oral statement of facts is drawing attention to key facts that will become important in subsequent arguments. The statement should be as short as possible to achieve the desired goal. In moot court situations, only the first speaker should state the facts, including facts important to the arguments of both teammates.

When representing the appellee, you must make a judgment call about how many facts to state. Undisputed facts stated by the appellant usually should not be repeated. However, the appellee can use a statement of facts to tell her own story, dispelling the vision of the case created by the appellant. Furthermore, if the appellee truly believes that the appellant has omitted or mischaracterized important facts, she can draw attention to these misrepresentations.

4. THE ARGUMENTS

You should present your strongest points early in the argument, using an "inverted pyramid" structure: begin with the most important and weighty arguments and end with the least. This order both attracts the court's attention and ensures that the most important points are not omitted if time runs out. As in the brief, you should always state conclusions first and then support them with facts and law. The opposite approach (setting out a series of premises that only later lead to conclusions) is often too complicated to be effective because judges will interrupt with questions before you have reached your point.

5. CONCLUSION

Whenever possible, try to save yourself enough time for a proper conclusion that will allow you to summarize your most important arguments. The conclusion should be a brief explanation of the relationship among all of the arguments presented, integrating them into your core theory. When there is nothing left to say and no further questions, thank the court and end the presentation, even if time is left. An attempt to fill the remaining time with a makeshift argument could distract the court or dilute the strength of your primary arguments.

B. ADDITIONAL CONSIDERATIONS SPECIFIC TO EACH PARTY

Given the format employed for oral argument, each party faces particular challenges. Depending on which party you represent, consider the following:

1. APPELLEE'S ARGUMENT

As the traditional appellee's argument is structurally similar to the appellant's, the guidelines listed above will be helpful. Appellee's counsel, just as much as appellant's, should develop an independent core theory, and should not limit herself entirely to a reactive role. However, the need to answer the appellant's arguments does create unique issues for the appellee. When the two sides explicitly disagree, the appellee may challenge the appellant's assertions directly. This affirmative method brings to sharp attention the distinctions between the two parties' cases. Counsel should listen closely to the appellant's oral presentation and to the questions the judges ask, taking notes as the argument proceeds. Although the appellee's counsel should have an outline prepared before the argument, she should also be ready to respond to any significant misrepresentations made by opposing counsel or to any issues that obviously concerned the judges when they questioned the other party.

2. Appellant's Rebuttal

At the beginning of the argument, the appellant may wish to reserve time for rebuttal. Rebuttal time should be used to clarify any prior arguments or respond to the appellee's presentation. Because it is the court's last impression of the case, rebuttal can be very important.

The time reserved for rebuttal should not be extensive, as reserving too much time may detract from the effectiveness of the main argument. In many circumstances, it may even be effective to decline the use of rebuttal time, indicating to the court that the case as first presented was solid and remains so even after the other side has presented its argument. An ill-prepared or rambling rebuttal can undermine even the best points made in the first argument. Rebuttals can also give the judges an opportunity to ask more difficult questions about the initial argument. Generally, rebuttal time should be used only to contest directly a point made by the appellee.

III. Questions by the Court

A. The Value of Questions

Questions from the court reveal the judges' perceptions of the case, as well as their biases and policy concerns. Listening carefully to the judges' questions and noticing their nonverbal cues make it easier to frame persuasive answers and to budget time. If it is apparent from the nods of the judges or from their questions that they already agree with your position on an issue, it may be a good idea to finish discussing that issue relatively soon and move on to a new issue. If the questions indicate that the court disagrees with certain contentions, you should take time to present arguments that might convince the court of the position's validity.

Not every question asked is meant to attack the position presented, so you should not assume that interruption for questions is a hostile act. Some questions are designed to support your view and some simply seek to clarify points about which the judge is confused and has no preconceived opinion. Furthermore, some "softball" questions are asked to allow the attorney to argue a point more fully. For example, a judge could ask the Bell-Wesleys' counsel:

> What policy goals would be served by allowing the Bell-Wesleys to recover child-rearing costs?

You should seize this chance to elucidate your position and impress a judge who is already an "ally." Do not miss the opportunity presented by a judge who offers you an open question, restates your argument in a new way, or supports your position with a new argument. Remember that a judge who agrees with you may be attempting to persuade the other panel members, so treat questions as an opportunity to shore up support for your client.

B. Effective Answering

1. Be Responsive

To respond to questions adequately, you must understand what the judge has asked. Always stop speaking when the judge interrupts you. If the question's wording is unclear, ask the judge to repeat or rephrase it. If the substantive implications of a question are unclear, repeat what the judge appears to be asking and inquire whether that is what the judge means. It is often wise to pause and reflect briefly on the question before beginning to speak. Taking a few seconds to collect your thoughts usually results in a more focused response. A prompt but disorganized answer may confuse the judge further, leading either to more questions or to a weak showing on the issue.

A judge's questions may spring from confusion; misunderstanding; concern about the consequences of broadening a legal rule; hostility born of a personal conviction that a position is wrong; or a genuine desire to help the speaker regain footing after a tough interrogation from a less-than-friendly colleague. Answers should be framed to address the judge's concerns, as evasive answers usually provoke judges to repeat questions and badger the speakers. In some cases, if a judge finds a party to be unduly evasive, she may grow exasperated and simply rule against that party. A judge also likes to think that her question is unique and will probably resent what sounds like a "pat" answer.

If the judge tries to elicit a "yes" or "no" response that seems to corner the speaker into a contrived position, the speaker should provide the one-word response but follow up quickly by explaining why the question is not so clear-cut; unwillingness to answer at all signals disrespect.

2. Advocate

You should use questions to advance your argument, even if the questions require bringing up a point before its planned place. Questions can also be used to put a positive spin on the client's position. You could make a concession, but show that it is not inconsistent with your client's case or that it is minor in comparison with the main point. You could also show that the judge's concern is even more reason to find for your client. Once the court seems satisfied with an answer, make a smooth transition from that response to another related topic and continue through your planned argument. Maintaining continuity and minimizing awkward silences is important, although a brief pause between arguments can be used advantageously.

Using a question as a vehicle to advance a line of argument is not an easy skill to master. The following is an example of how an attorney for the appellant in *Bell-Wesley v. O'Toole* might proceed.

> **Sample question and answer:**
>
> *Judge*: If the Bell-Wesleys didn't want to pay child-rearing costs, why did they conceive children on three prior occasions?
>
> *Appellants' attorney*: Your Honor, it may seem logical that if the Bell-Wesleys were prepared to assume the financial burden of raising children in the past, there is no reason they should not be similarly situated now. Before experiencing the tremendous emotional

> anguish accompanying the births and deaths of three deformed children, the Bell-Wesleys had indeed decided to take on the financial burden of raising children. However, after suffering immeasurably when each of their children died in infancy, they made a conscious choice to forego having children. Once they made that decision, they no longer accounted for children in their financial decisions and long-term planning. The issue is not whether, since they previously conceived and gave birth to children, they should now be presumed to be in the same financial position to raise Frank Michael. Rather, the issue is whether Dr. O'Toole's negligence caused the Bell-Wesleys a financial loss. Dr. O'Toole gave the Bell-Wesleys reason to believe that they would not have children and could plan their life accordingly. Dr. O'Toole must be held liable for all the foreseeable consequences of his negligence, including the costs of raising a healthy child to majority.

The first sentence of this sample answer restates the question. By restating the question counsel has shown that she fully understands the question asked. (Indeed, the judge could have interrupted and corrected any misperception of the question.) Then, counsel uses the question as a platform to advance her argument that damages ought to be awarded; to remind the judge of the Bell-Wesleys' personal suffering; and to reframe the question from "Why did the parents attempt to have children before?" to "What responsibility does Dr. O'Toole have for his negligence now?"

Good preparation is the key to answering questions. Although it is natural to feel unprepared and apprehensive going into oral argument, an advocate who has reviewed the record, authorities, and briefs will often be pleasantly surprised and find that the court's questions are manageable. Finally, if there seems to be no good answer to a question, be very honest with the court. Being evasive is more detrimental than simply saying, "I don't know."

3. BE SENSITIVE TO THE TYPES OF QUESTIONS ASKED

When responding to questions from the judges, try to concentrate on the central thrust of their inquiry. Generally, questions focus on one of the following concerns: the facts, the policy considerations, the cited authorities, or the legal arguments. Each category of questions calls for a different type of response.

Generally, when a judge asks about the facts of the case, she is looking to move from abstract legal principles to a concrete application of the law to the current case. In this situation, you should provide explicit facts and citations to the record in a framework conducive to your side of the case.

In contrast, questions about policy concerns are generally looking for arguments arising from information outside the facts of the current case. Here, a judge is likely seeking a better understanding of the potential consequences of her decision.

Questions about cited authorities typically call for more than the simple facts and holding of a case. Instead, the judge wants to know how the authority relates to the case being argued. Is it binding in this jurisdiction? Does it show an existing framework of law into which the desired result must fit? Can a valid and consistent exception to the precedent be made without detracting from the force of the precedent as a whole? In response, you should focus on telling the judge why a particular precedent is controlling, persuasive, and based in sound policy.

Finally, questions about the legal arguments often focus on hypothetical situations to test the limits and illustrate the implications of the legal principle argued. Be sure that you are completely comfortable with your arguments and their limits if you want to avoid being tricked into supporting a legal argument that has absurd outcomes. If you find yourself being drawn into far-reaching hypotheticals and slippery slope arguments, remember that the case being argued involves specific parties in a single fact situation. Weaving the facts neatly into your answers can help prevent you from getting trapped into defending a broad general principle against all possible attacks.

C. Questioning in Team Situations

Although judges should refrain from questioning one member of the team about issues for which the other member is primarily responsible, each co-counsel should understand her partner's basic arguments. If questioning becomes too specific, ask the court either to permit co-counsel to return to the lectern or, in the case of the first oralist, to await your teammate's later appearance. If properly prepared, the second speaker may also take the opportunity to cover crucial points that her co-counsel inadvertently omitted and to develop further any answers that may have been inadequate.

IV. Presenting the Oral Argument

A. Be Yourself

If there is one general rule of presenting an oral argument, it is "be yourself." An ordinarily even-tempered and moderate person usually should not affect a flashy, fist-pounding display of rhetoric. Trying too hard to create a different, "effective" personality for the argument diverts your energy and attention away from the issues in the case, and it can be hard to maintain. There is no single right way to argue a case, and the more comfortable you are, the more effective the argument is likely to be. You should assess your personality and speaking style ahead of time and think of ways to use your unique strengths in the argument and to polish your own delivery.

B. Effective Delivery

A clear presentation that is easy to follow is crucial in oral argument. The general rules of effective public speaking apply equally well to oral arguments; speak loudly enough to be heard, and slowly enough to be understood. You should not read from notes unless absolutely necessary, because a paper barrier between the court and counsel inhibits effective presentation. The best advocates have a thorough knowledge of relevant materials. This does not mean memorizing case citations. Rather, it means dealing quickly and surely with the issues and calling forth relevant arguments without fumbling through a mound of written materials for a case or fact. Eye contact with the judges is extremely helpful, both in terms of keeping the judges focused on you and convincing them that the argument is defensible. With good eye contact, you are most likely to involve the judges in an active process.

Quoting cases to support arguments is sometimes useful, but quotes should be short and used sparingly if at all. In general, paraphrasing the language of cases cited in the brief is a more effective way of communicating their essence to the judges and a more efficient use of time.

The most effective oral arguments have the tone of a conversation rather than a speech. In this way, oral argument is quite different from a presentation to a jury. It need not be as heightened or dramatized as a statement before a jury, partially because the judges know the applicable law thoroughly, and partially because judges may interrupt you. Still, within this conversation, you should remember that your goal is to persuade and to get across a point of view. Toward that end, you should speak clearly and convey your belief in what you are arguing.

You should avoid legalese and other jargon when there is a simpler way to make your point. Overly complex sentence structure may make your argument hard to follow. Remember that a person's attention span when listening to a speaker is significantly less than when reading a brief. Therefore, it is useful preparation to take an especially complicated sentence from the brief and figure out how to express it orally by colloquializing it, simplifying it, and imbuing it with feeling without becoming too informal.

To some extent the conversational character of a presentation will depend on how many questions the judges ask. But regardless of the behavior of the judges, remember that oral argument is still an exercise in public speaking and should be treated as such. Speak clearly, projecting your voice towards the judges. Speak a little more slowly than you would in everyday conversation to make sure you do not mumble or swallow the ends of your sentence. Keep your delivery interesting by varying your tone and cadence to emphasize key words and concepts. Pausing for emphasis, if used sparingly, can also be powerful. Finally, be aware of your body language. Maintain eye contact with the judges and try to minimize distracting movements like pen-clicking or nervous hand motions. When kept to a minimum, gestures can become more effective as a means to emphasize the key sections of your argument.

It is unrealistic to expect to be allowed to deliver a complete prepared speech. In fact, the procedural rules for the federal appellate courts prohibit the reading of briefs at argument. Some speakers feel most comfortable after writing out at least the first minute (about a page) of their argument. Although reading this introduction may make the opening moments easier, counsel usually should resist the temptation to read. Use notes as a back-up, but focus on talking to the judges and maintaining eye contact.

C. Attitude Toward the Court

Your attitude toward the court should be one of respectful equality: you should not be servile to the court, but you should accord judges due deference. Even in the heat of hard questioning, you should be receptive and cooperative. If a particular judge or question annoys you, do not show it. Giving definite answers to the court's questions, speaking with an animated and positive tone, and being confident in the strength of your argument is more likely to promote listening than adopting an aggressive interpersonal manner. Hostile behavior can be perceived as "defensive" and may suggest that you are unable to support your own argument.

You should attempt to be helpful to the court and to make sure everything is clear. You should not treat anything as obvious or as a waste of time, but rather you should act as a true "counselor" and respond empathetically to judges' concerns. Of course, once you have answered a question, you can indicate politely but firmly that you will now move on to the next point.

A few customs of formal conduct should be observed in oral argument. The customs do not vary much from courtroom to courtroom. When beginning the argument, speakers should rise and say, "May it please the court," or "If the court pleases," before introducing themselves. In answering questions, address the judge as "Your Honor." In referring to members of the court, "Judge Smith" or "The Chief Justice" is appropriate. Opposing counsel should be referred to as such, or as "Mr. Neuville" or "counsel for the defendant" but never as "my opponent." Associate counsel is called "my colleague," "my associate," "co-counsel," or "Ms. Harvey."

D. Handling Miscitations and Misrepresentations by Opposing Counsel

Bring any miscitations and misrepresentations of opposing counsel to the court's attention when they are important to the case. If a misrepresentation influences an essential argument; if the court will be unable to find the correct citation; or if the judges' questions reveal that they do not realize that a fact or doctrine has been misrepresented, you should call attention to the misrepresentation. When appropriate, corrections can help your credibility. However, you should not appear to be attacking opposing counsel personally. For instance, an advocate in the *Bell-Wesley* case might say:

> It appears that opposing counsel is claiming that Dr. O'Toole guaranteed the 100% effectiveness of the vasectomy. If the Court would please refer to Exhibit 4 in the record, the Court will see that the Bell-Wesleys signed an acknowledgment that Dr. O'Toole had informed them of the chance that any given vasectomy would not be successful.

V. How to End Gracefully and Persuasively

Oral argument is not a natural exercise for most first-year law students. It is full of procedural requirements and formality that you may not have been exposed to before law school. But this does not mean that the task must be a daunting one. With adequate preparation and a bit of practice, oral argument can become an opportunity to showcase the hard work you have put into refining your argument and to demonstrate how well you know your case.

The best oral advocates will often be those who have mastered their party's position so well that they can speak about it naturally and compellingly. While a feeling of nervousness is almost inevitable, knowledge of your facts, cases, and arguments will reduce the opportunities for you to be caught off guard. The better prepared you are, the more oral argument can start to resemble a conversation. After all the time you have spent researching your case and writing your brief, it can be very gratifying—and even fun—to engage with respected judges on a subject you know so well.

Once you have completed your argument, remind the court what action you would like it to take (e.g., "we therefore ask that you affirm the

Superior Court's judgment"), thank the court, and take your seat. And, when you leave the courtroom and have a moment, congratulate yourself on your achievement. You learned how to organize legal writing, how to synthesize rules, how to conduct legal research, how to draft predictive and persuasive legal writing, how to approach a case and develop a core theory, and how to present an oral argument. These are all tremendous accomplishments, and though you will spend your career honing these skills, you are well on your way to becoming a skilled legal advocate.

APPENDIX A

Sample Assigning Materials

Date: October 8, 2012
Subject: New case
To: leagalintern@cffaf.org
From: joe.smith@cffaf.org

Hey there—

Sorry I haven't stopped by yet; I've been caught up in that wiretap litigation. I hope you're settling into the fellowship well. I have a new case I was hoping you could help me out with. My high school friend Betsy Schmidt called a few weeks ago in a panic. She was served with a complaint in a lawsuit filed against her by another friend of ours. We all went to high school in southern California. Betsy now lives in the San Francisco Bay Area. The plaintiff, Luke Baird, now lives in Chicago. He filed suit in the United States District Court for the Northern District of Illinois. Luke alleges that Betsy defamed him in a posting on the website "lovehimorleavehim.com," which contains reviews and feedback on online dating profiles. Betsy is a grad student and can't afford to travel to Illinois to defend this suit, or really even to hire an attorney. So I told her I'd see what we could do. As you may know, more and more people are getting sued for what they post on the Internet.

I think we can probably win on the merits. Betsy tells me that she and Luke had an affair last year, lasting eight months and ending around the time of Luke's wedding. She says that everything she said in the posting is true. It's undisputed that Luke had an active online dating profile on the website "perfectmatch.com" while he was engaged. Additionally, lovehimorleavehim.com warns that material posted on the site might be "offensive or objectionable."

But I really don't want to have to get to the merits in this case because it would be so difficult on Betsy. Because Betsy has had virtually no contact with Illinois, I think we have a good argument that the court doesn't have personal jurisdiction here. I've made a few calls, and all of lovehimorleavehim's operations are based out of California too. Both its server and its offices are located in the Bay Area. Of course, Luke could still file a new suit in California, but it's worth taking a chance that he won't take the case that far.

After I read the complaint, I called Luke's attorney to see if they'd voluntarily dismiss the case. But she said neither she nor Luke was interested in cooperating, so I guess we'll have to go to court. She did tell me, though, that they're not pursuing a general jurisdiction argument. They're going to argue that the posting itself gave rise to specific jurisdiction over Betsy.

I'd like you to write me a memo assessing whether we would be successful in filing a motion to dismiss the case for lack of personal jurisdiction. In drafting your memo, please focus solely on whether Betsy Schmidt has established sufficient "minimum contacts" with Illinois such that the exercise of personal jurisdiction over her is proper. I am having another staffer look into the issue of whether the exercise of personal jurisdiction over Schmidt would violate "fair play and substantial justice"—so you can ignore that part of the analysis.

I've attached an affidavit from Betsy that we could use to support a motion to dismiss. I'm pretty sure Illinois is one of the states with a long-arm statute that permits the courts to exercise jurisdiction to the maximum extent allowed by Due Process, but you'll want to look at how Illinois courts have been applying that statute lately.

—JOE

Joe Smith

Director

Center for First Amendment Freedoms

www.cffaf.org

NOTICE: This communication may contain privileged or other confidential information. If you have received it in error, please advise the sender by reply email and immediately delete the message and any attachments without copying or disclosing the contents. Thank you.

United States District Court
Northern District of Illinois

LUKE BAIRD,	)	
Plaintiff,	)	
vs.	)	Case No.: No. CV-06-55555
BETSY SCHMIDT	)	COMPLAINT
	)	DEMAND FOR JURY TRIAL
and	)	
LOVEHIMORLEAVEHIM, INC.,	)	
a Delaware corporation,	)	
Defendants.	)	

Luke Baird, by and through his attorneys, Hallgreen and Silver, LLP, hereby submits this Complaint and Jury Demand, and in support of, states the following:

PARTIES, JURISDICTION, AND VENUE

1. Plaintiff, Luke Baird, is a citizen of the United States and is domiciled in the state of Illinois. Mr. Baird has been domiciled in the state of Illinois at all times relevant to the incidents described herein.

2. Defendant Betsy Schmidt is a citizen of the United States and is domiciled in the state of California. Ms. Schmidt has been domiciled in California at all times relevant to the incidents described herein.

3. Defendant Lovehimorleavehim, Inc., is a Delaware corporation with its principal place of business in Menlo Park, California. It has been publishing information about Illinois residents since 2005.

4. Jurisdiction in this Court is proper pursuant to 28 U.S.C. § 1332, diversity of citizenship, as the matter in controversy exceeds $75,000 and is between citizens of different states.

5. Venue is appropriate in this Court pursuant to 28 U.S.C. § 1391(a).

FACTUAL ALLEGATIONS

6. Defendant Lovehimorleavehim maintains a website that it describes as "a community for truth in dating." According to its FAQs page, lovehimorleavehim.com "is a community Web site where you can post and read reviews about the truthfulness of profiles on online dating sites like Match.com, Yahoo Personals, and MySpace as well as meet other online daters to share information and stories. Lovehimorleavehim.com is free and anonymous to use."

7. The website contains profiles of more than 5000 men and receives 100 new submissions per day. At least 200 of the profiles are of individuals allegedly located in Illinois.

8. The website averages 300,000 visitors per day.

9. Defendant Lovehimorleavehim candidly admits that it does "not actively monitor use of [its] discussion groups, bulletin boards or chat rooms."

10. Plaintiff is a post-doctoral fellow doing cancer research in a biology laboratory at the University of Chicago. He is currently applying for jobs as an assistant professor at universities across the country.

11. Plaintiff and his colleagues depend on grant money from foundations and the federal government to fund their work. Plaintiff's good reputation is essential to his occupation.

12. Plaintiff has an excellent reputation for honesty and integrity in both his business and personal affairs.

13. Plaintiff was married to Denise Ma on May 27, 2012, in a ceremony on the island of Kauai, Hawaii.

14. On or about May 24, 2012, Defendant Betsy Schmidt published an anonymous "profile" on lovehimorleavehim.com.

15. The "profile" included a picture of Plaintiff and identified him by name.

16. Among other things, the posting falsely accused Plaintiff of cheating on his now-wife and stealing money from the University of Chicago. A true and correct copy of the "profile" is attached as Exhibit A.

17. The "profile" could be located by searching the lovehimorleavehim.com website by Plaintiff's name or by browsing all profiles from Illinois.

18. In accordance with its customary practice, Defendant Lovehimorleavehim did nothing to independently verify the information contained in the posting.

19. The profile allows others to either post public responses or email the poster directly.

20. In a public reply, one reader indicated that Plaintiff "should be ashamed of [him]self" and "deserve[s] whatever [he] get[s]."

21. The website allows readers to forward the profiles to personal email accounts.

22. On or about June 1, 2012, an unknown individual forwarded the hyperlink to the profile to Plaintiff's now-wife.

23. Upon learning of the posting, Plaintiff requested Defendants Schmidt and Lovehimorleavehim to remove it from the website. Both defendants refused to remove the defamatory statement from the website.

24. As a result of the posting, Plaintiff has had to move out of the home he shares with his wife and rent an apartment.

25. Plaintiff and his wife are seeking marital counseling, but the damage to the relationship may be irreparable.

26. On or about June 1, 2012, an unknown individual forwarded the posting to Plaintiff's supervisor at the University of Chicago.

27. As a result of the posting, the University of Chicago has placed Plaintiff on unpaid leave and launched an investigation into his business expenses.

28. Pending the resolution of the investigation, Plaintiff's advisors at the University of Chicago have refused to serve as references for his job applications.

COUNT I (against both Defendants)

29. Plaintiff hereby incorporates paragraphs 1 through 20 above as if set forth in their entirety.

30. As set forth above, Defendants published false and defamatory statements regarding Plaintiff.

31. These statements constituted defamation by libel and slander under Illinois law.

32. Defendants published the defamatory statements with knowledge of the falsity of the statements and/or with reckless disregard as to the truth of the statements.

33. Defendants failed properly to investigate the subject matter of the defamatory statements prior to publishing them.

34. The postings violated Defendant Lovehimorleavehim's terms of use, including a prohibition on content that is "defamatory [or] offensive."

35. As a direct and proximate result of Defendants' conduct, Plaintiff has suffered embarrassment, humiliation, and emotional distress that may be permanent in nature.

36. As a direct and proximate result of Defendants' conduct, Plaintiff has suffered damage to his reputation, which may be permanent in nature.

37. As a direct and proximate result of Defendants' conduct, Plaintiff's earning capacity has been impaired and/or may be impaired in the future.

PRAYER AND REQUEST FOR RELIEF

Plaintiff seeks all relief provided for by law, including, but not limited to compensatory damages in excess of $200,000, and such other and further relief as the Court deems just, proper, and equitable.

PLAINTIFF HEREBY DEMANDS A JURY TRIAL ON ALL ISSUES OF FACT.

Dated this 14th day of September, 2012,

Laurie M. Hallgreen

Laurie M. Hallgreen
Hallgreen & Silver, LLP
123 Rocky Drive, Suite 42
Chicago, Illinois 60601

EXHIBIT A

Luke Baird   http://www.lovehimorleavehim.com/index-dev.php?action=read-review&x=drlove

Love him ♡ or leave him? 💔

Profile: drlove
Site: Perfectmatch.com
Real name: Luke Baird
Gender: Male
Location: Illinois, California, Maryland, Washington
Date Added: 5/24/2012

Reviews on Profile: drlove (Perfectmatch.com)

He is a lying, cheating bastard who is sleeping with a girl he's known since his days at University High School even though he left tonight for his wedding and honeymoon in Kauai. His new wife Denise is a teacher at the Latin School. (Did he think I wouldn't ever put that knowledge to good use? I hope someone lets her know about him, but it won't be me.). His profile says he's a professor but he's really just a post-doc at the University of Chicago and has been using university time and money to conduct an extramarital affair while on business trips. (Of course I didn't mind the lovely week in Seattle when he was doing research at the University of Washington Medical Center; it was quite nice of him to pay for the hotel room and the meals.) He is incapable of anything but lying and cheating: cheating on the woman who is going to be his wife, cheating his lab out of money, and cheating me out of my best friend.

United States District Court
Northern District of Illinois

LUKE BAIRD,	)	
Plaintiff,	)	
vs.	)	
BETSY SCHMIDT	)	Case No.: No. CV-06-55555
and	)	
LOVEHIMORLEAVEHIM,	)	
a Delaware corporation,	)	
Defendants.	)	

AFFIDAVIT OF BETSY SCHMIDT

1. I first met Luke Baird when we attended the same elementary school for third grade. We went to school together through high school.

2. During the time we were in school together, we never dated or had a sexual relationship.

3. We did not keep in touch regularly after graduating in 2001.

4. I now live in Oakland, California and am a doctoral student in French Literature at the University of California, Berkeley.

5. In June 2011, I placed a profile on the online dating site perfectmatch.com, indicating that I was interested in meeting men living in the Bay Area.

6. In August 2011, I received a message from Mr. Baird through the website. His user name was "drlove." He claimed he was a single college professor in Illinois who traveled regularly to San Francisco, Los Angeles, Seattle, and Baltimore for research.

7. Mr. Baird came to town on a business trip in approximately September 2011 and asked me to dinner. After dinner he suggested I return to his hotel room with him. We engaged in consensual sexual relations in the hotel room that evening.

8. After that day, I communicated with Mr. Baird several times each day by phone, email, and instant message. Sometimes these conversations lasted several hours.

9. I do not recall when I first learned that he was engaged to be married.

10. Because Mr. Baird travels for work a great deal, I never knew where he was when I was communicating with him.

11. On three other occasions between September 2011 and April 2012, Mr. Baird came to town and stayed in my apartment, rather than in a hotel.

12. On one occasion in February 2012, Mr. Baird bought me a plane ticket to Seattle, where he was going on a business trip. I stayed with him in his hotel room.

13. Throughout the period September 2011 through April 2012, Mr. Baird told me every day that he was in love with me. On more than one occasion he told me that he wanted to marry me.

14. I believed Mr. Baird was planning to leave his fiancée to be with me, and I removed my profile from the perfectmatch.com website.

15. When Mr. Baird left for his wedding in Hawaii, I had not heard from him for two days, and I was devastated.

16. I visited the perfectmatch.com website and discovered that he had never removed his profile. In fact, he had been active on the site within the previous 24 hours.

17. I finally realized that Mr. Baird was a liar and a manipulator, and I wanted to alert other women to his lies.

18. I posted a profile on lovehimorleavehim.com, identifying him by name, supplying a picture, and describing his lies.

19. I identified his locations as California, Illinois, Maryland, and Washington, based on the locations in his perfectmatch.com profile.

20. Everything in the posting is true.

21. Before submitting the profile, I agreed, by clicking an "accept" button, to the following terms:

   a. "I am at least 18 years old.

   b. I will not post any defamatory, inaccurate, abusive, obscene, profane, offensive, sexually oriented, threatening, harassing, racially offensive, or illegal material, or any material that infringes or violates another party's rights (including, but not limited to, intellectual property rights, and rights of privacy and publicity).

   c. By clicking on the 'accept' button below, I will have released Lovehimorleavehim, Inc. from any liability that may arise from my use of the site."

22. Before submitting the profile, I also agreed, by clicking an "accept" button that "[t]he Terms and the relationship between you and Lovehimorleavehim, Inc. shall be governed by the laws of the State of California without regard to its conflict of law provisions. You and Lovehimorleavehim, Inc. agree to submit to the personal and exclusive jurisdiction of the courts located within the county of San Mateo, California."

23. I emailed the posting to five friends, three in California, one in Indiana, and one in Massachusetts. I did not ask any of them to forward it to anyone else. I did not email the posting to any other individuals.

24. I do not know who forwarded the posting to Mr. Baird's wife.

25. I do not know who forwarded the posting to individuals at the University of Chicago.

26. I have never been to visit Illinois. I do not own any property in Illinois. I do not have any contracts with anyone in Illinois.

27. My only income is from working as a teaching assistant and barely covers my monthly bills.

Betsy Schmidt

Betsy Schmidt

Dated: October 2, 2012

Personally appeared before me the above-named Betsy Schmidt and made oath that the foregoing statements are made upon personal knowledge and are true.

Pat Blake

Pat Blake
Notary Public

APPENDIX B

Sample Predictive Memorandum

MEMORANDUM

TO: Joe Smith
FROM: Legal Intern
DATE: November 17, 2012
CASE: Luke Baird v. Betsy Schmidt; file number 0928–78
RE: Internet jurisdiction: motion to dismiss due to lack of minimum contacts

QUESTION PRESENTED

Luke Baird, an Illinois resident, has filed a complaint against Betsy Schmidt in the Northern District of Illinois alleging defamation through a posting on lovehimorleavehim.com. In the posting, Schmidt accused Baird of conducting an extramarital affair while on business trips. The posting was forwarded via email to Baird's wife and employer in Illinois. By posting the accusation, has Schmidt established sufficient minimum contacts with Illinois such that the court may exercise personal jurisdiction over her?

BRIEF ANSWER

Probably yes. Under the Due Process Clause as interpreted by the Supreme Court and the Seventh Circuit, a non-resident defendant establishes minimum contacts with a forum by committing an (1) intentional act which is (2) expressly aimed at the forum and (3) causes harm, the brunt of which is suffered—and which the defendant knows is likely to be suffered—in the forum. Schmidt's intentional posting of the statements is not in dispute, and she expressly aimed her actions at the forum by referencing Illinois in her posting, identifying Baird's Illinois employers, and inciting readers to contact Baird's wife. The court will presume that the harm has accrued in Illinois since that is where Baird resides. Because Schmidt knew that Baird lived and worked in Illinois and refused to remove the posting, she knew or should have known that her actions would likely harm Baird in Illinois. Thus, the court will likely find that Schmidt established minimum contacts with Illinois such that it is entitled to exercise personal jurisdiction over her.

FACTS

On May 24th, 2012, Defendant Betsy Schmidt ("Schmidt"), a California resident, posted an anonymous profile page about Illinois resident Plaintiff Luke Baird ("Baird") on the lovehimorleavehim.com website. Compl. ¶ 14; Schmidt Aff. ¶ 18; Baird Ex. A. Lovehimorleavehim.com, Inc. ("Lovehimorleavehim"), an online "community for truth in dating," provides a forum for users to post comments about the truthfulness of personal dating profiles located on other websites. Compl. ¶ 6. Schmidt's posting—which included Baird's photograph, full name, and "perfectmatch.com" username of "drlove"—referred to Baird as a "lying cheating bastard," and accused him of conducting an affair with Schmidt while he was engaged to another woman. Baird Ex. A. In addition to its account of Baird's infidelity to his then-fiancée and current wife, Schmidt's posting also described Baird's questionable business practices of using research grants from his post-doctoral fellowship at the University of Chicago to fund trips taken with Schmidt. Id. According to Schmidt, she created the posting on lovehimorleavehim.com in order to "alert other women to [Baird's] lies." Schmidt Aff. ¶ 17.

None of the material events referenced in Schmidt's posting occurred in Illinois. See id. at ¶¶ 7–12; Baird Ex. A. Schmidt and Baird first met during elementary school in California, Schmidt Aff. ¶ 1, and during the course of their affair, they only spent time together in California and Washington, id. at ¶¶ 7, 11–12. Nevertheless, the posting did mention Baird's wife, Denise, by name along with Denise's employment at the Latin School in Chicago. Baird Ex. A. Schmidt wrote, "I hope someone lets her know about him. . . ." Id. The posting also described Baird's employment as a post-doctoral fellow at the University of Chicago, id., while listing Illinois, California, Maryland, and Washington as the posting's relevant locations, id. Schmidt claims that she selected these locations because they were the locations that Baird himself had listed on his perfectmatch.com profile. Schmidt Aff. ¶ 19.

Lovehimorleavehim is a Delaware corporation with its principal place of business in Menlo Park, California. Compl. ¶ 3. Although the website is accessible worldwide, users may search the profile pages on the website by their listed geographic locations. Id. at ¶ 17. At least 200 of the profile pages located on lovehimorleavehim.com feature individuals located in Illinois. Id. at ¶ 7. The website, which averages 300,000 visitors per day, id. at ¶ 8, allows users to create and post profile pages, respond publicly to profiles, and to email the poster directly, id. at ¶ 19.

After Schmidt created and submitted the profile page on lovehimorleavehim.com, she e-mailed a hyperlink to the page to five friends, none of whom lived in Illinois. Schmidt Aff. ¶ 23. Schmidt did not ask any of her friends to forward the hyperlink to anyone else, but someone did forward the link to Baird's wife in Illinois and to Baird's supervisors at the University of Chicago. Compl. ¶¶ 22, 26. As a result, Baird has experienced harm to both his marriage and his career. See id. at ¶¶ 25, 27–28. He has been forced to move out of the home he once shared with his wife. Id. at ¶ 24. In addition, Baird's supervisors at the University of Chicago have commenced an investigation into his business expenses, placed him on unpaid leave, and refused to serve as references for his nation-wide job search. Id. at ¶¶ 27–28. Baird has now filed suit in the Northern District of Illinois alleging that Schmidt's profile page constitutes defamation under Illinois law. See Compl. ¶ 31. Schmidt contacted us asking for advice, and she is hoping to pursue a motion to dismiss the case for lack of personal jurisdiction.

DISCUSSION

The court will probably find that Schmidt established minimum contacts with Illinois sufficient for the court to assert specific personal jurisdiction over her. A federal court may exert personal jurisdiction over Schmidt only if Illinois state courts may do so. See Fed. R. Civ. P. 4(k)(1)(A). Under Illinois's long-arm statute, Illinois state courts may "exercise jurisdiction on any . . . basis . . . permitted by the Illinois Constitution and the Constitution of the United States." 735 Ill. Comp. Stat. 5/2-209(c) (2012). The Seventh Circuit has interpreted this catch-all provision as authorizing jurisdiction to the extent allowed by the United States Constitution. See Hyatt Int'l Corp. v. Coco, 302 F.3d 707, 714–15 (7th Cir. 2002). Thus, it is sufficient to evaluate whether the exercise of personal jurisdiction over Schmidt would comport with the Due Process Clause of the Fourteenth Amendment. In International Shoe Co. v. Washington, 326 U.S. 310 (1945), the Supreme Court held that Due Process requires that a defendant establish certain "minimum contacts" with the forum before a court may assert specific personal jurisdiction over the defendant.

The Supreme Court applied International Shoe's minimum contacts doctrine to a defamation suit in Calder v. Jones, 465 U.S. 783 (1984). In Calder, a California actress brought suit in California against a writer of a national magazine based in Florida. The Court held that personal jurisdiction was proper because of the "effects" in California of the writer's Florida conduct. See id. at 789. The Seventh Circuit's interpretations of Calder in Wallace v. Herron, 778 F.2d 391 (7th Cir. 1985), Indianapolis Colts v. Metro Baltimore Football Club, L.P., 34 F.3d 410 (7th Cir. 1994), and Janmark, Inc. v. Reidy, 132 F.3d 1200 (7th Cir. 1997) are somewhat ill-defined and potentially conflicting. However, the Northern District of Illinois has read into the Seventh Circuit's holdings an implicit Calder "effects test," suggesting that the court will likely apply all three prongs of the test to Schmidt's case. In order to satisfy the Calder effects test, a defendant must: (1) commit intentional tortious actions; (ii) expressly aimed at Illinois; (iii) which cause harm to the plaintiff in Illinois that the defendant knows is likely to be suffered in Illinois. See Euromarket Designs, Inc. v. Crate & Barrel Ltd., 96 F. Supp. 2d 824, 835 (N.D. Ill. 2000).

This memo will first discuss the Northern District of Illinois's interpretation of Seventh Circuit precedent applying the Calder effects test. This memo will then argue that because Schmidt intentionally posted the allegedly defamatory statements, the first prong of the effects test is not in dispute. It will then show that Schmidt's actions were expressly aimed at Illinois. Finally, the memo will demonstrate that Schmidt knew or should have known that Baird was likely to suffer personal and professional harm in Illinois as a proximate result of her actions. Thus, the court will probably find that Schmidt established minimum contacts with Illinois such that the exercise of personal jurisdiction over her is proper.

I. The Northern District of Illinois has interpreted potentially inconsistent Seventh Circuit precedent as requiring a defendant to satisfy all three prongs of the Calder effects test

The "[r]elevant jurisprudence of the Seventh Circuit has not been consistent in the verbiage used to determine personal jurisdiction." Caterpillar Inc. v. Miskin Scraper Works, Inc., 256 F. Supp. 2d 849, 851 (C.D. Ill. 2003). Strikingly, the Seventh Circuit's most recent application of Calder appeared to forsake the "express aiming" prong of the effects test. See Janmark, 132 F.3d at 1202. In Janmark, the court found that the exercise of personal jurisdiction in Illinois over a non-resident defendant was proper on the basis of a single telephone call made by the defendant in California to one of the Illinois plaintiff's customers in New Jersey. See id. Because the defendant's call allegedly caused the New Jersey customer to cancel his purchase of miniature shopping carts from the plaintiff, the court held that the "injury"—and thus the intentional tort—had "occurred" in Illinois. See id. Finding the location of the injury dispositive, the court wrote, "there can be no serious doubt after Calder that the state in which the victim of a tort suffers the injury may entertain a suit against the accused tortfeasor." Id. Thus, the Janmark court appeared to interpret Calder so broadly that virtually any tort causing harm to an Illinois plaintiff would justify personal jurisdiction over the defendant.

However, the Janmark court did not explicitly overrule Seventh Circuit precedent, and the Northern District of Illinois has not adopted Janmark's broad interpretation of Calder. The Seventh Circuit had previously rejected the assertion that a victim's place of injury by itself can serve as a sufficient basis for the exercise of personal jurisdiction over a non-resident tortfeasor. See Wallace, 778 F.2d at 394 ("[w]e do not believe the Supreme Court, in Calder, was saying that any plaintiff may hale any defendant into court in the plaintiff's home state, where the defendant has no contacts, merely by asserting that the defendant has committed an intentional tort against the plaintiff").

In Indianapolis Colts, the court refused to base its finding of personal jurisdiction solely on a showing that the injurious "effects" of the defendant's alleged infringement of the plaintiff's trademark occurred in the forum state. 34 F.3d at 412. Rather than rest on "so austere a conception" of personal jurisdiction, the court held that the defendant Baltimore Colts football team could be forced to defend itself against the plaintiff's suit in Indiana because "the defendant had done *more than* brought about an injury to an interest located in a particular state." Id. (emphasis added). Not only had the defendant harmed the plaintiff in Indiana by infringing its trademark, but also the defendant had " 'entered' the state" through its nationwide television broadcasts of Baltimore Colts football games. Id.

On its face, the "entry" requirement of Indianapolis Colts appears to conflict with Janmark's unqualified assertion that anyone who intentionally causes a tortious injury in Illinois is amenable to suit there. See Caterpillar, 256 F. Supp. 2d at 851–52 (describing the tension between Janmark and Indianapolis Colts). However, since Janmark, district courts in the Seventh Circuit have resolved this linguistic discrepancy by equating the "entry" requirement of Indianapolis Colts with "express aiming." See, e.g., id. at 852; Richter v. INSTAR Enters. Int'l, 594 F. Supp. 2d 1000, 1010 (N.D. Ill. 2009); Nerds on Call, Inc. v. Nerds on Call, Inc., 598 F. Supp. 2d 913, 917, 919 (S.D. Ind. 2008).

In other words, regardless of whether it is characterized as "entry" into the forum state or as "intentional and purposeful tortious conduct . . . calculated to cause injury in the forum state," Caterpillar, 256 F. Supp. 2d at 851, there must be some "express aiming" at the forum state—in addition to mere "effects" suffered by a resident of the forum—in order for a court to assert personal jurisdiction over a non-resident tortfeasor. See id. Thus, despite the varying language used, courts in the Northern District of Illinois have all adopted some version of the traditional three-factor "effects test."

II. Schmidt's posting satisfies each prong of the Calder effects test
A. Schmidt intentionally posted the online profile

In Illinois, under the effects test, personal jurisdiction over a nonresident defendant first requires that the defendant commit "intentional tortious actions." Euromarket, 96 F. Supp. 2d at 835. Defamation is an intentional tort. See Calder, 465 U.S. at 789–90. Schmidt does not dispute that she intentionally posted the statements. See Schmidt Aff. ¶ 18. Additionally, in judging the motion to dismiss, the court will resolve any conflicts in the affidavits in the plaintiff's favor. RAR, Inc. v. Turner Diesel, Ltd., 107

F.3d 1272, 1275 (7th Cir. 1997). Thus, the court will accept as true Baird's allegations of defamation and hold that Schmidt has satisfied the first prong of the test.

B. Schmidt "expressly aimed" the posting at Illinois

Under Illinois law, the second prong of the effects test requires that a defendant "expressly aim" her actions at Illinois. Euromarket, 96 F. Supp. 2d at 835. In assessing whether a defendant has "expressly aimed" her tortious activity at the forum state, courts determine whether the forum state is the focal point of the activity, such that the alleged defamatory statements involve conduct, people, and events in the forum. See, e.g., Jackson v. Cal. Newspapers P'ship, 406 F. Supp. 2d 893, 897 (N.D. Ill. 2005). In Jackson, the court refused to exercise jurisdiction over a defendant newspaper publisher on the basis of an online article that allegedly defamed multi-sport professional athlete Vincent E. ("Bo") Jackson. The defendant's article on the "dangers of steroid abuse"—which mentioned that Jackson had lost his hip as a result of his use of anabolic steroids—was deemed insufficient to confer personal jurisdiction because "the defendants did not contact Illinois sources, did not focus the story on Illinois or any event that occurred in Illinois, and did not know that the plaintiff resided in Illinois." Jackson, 406 F. Supp. 2d at 896.

Other courts have similarly declined to find jurisdiction on the basis of defamatory articles where the forum state was not the "focal point of the article." See, e.g., Revell v. Lidov, 317 F.3d 467, 473 (5th Cir. 2002) (holding that the court lacked jurisdiction over non-resident defendants in Texas where the defendants' allegedly defamatory online posting "contain[ed] no reference to Texas, nor . . . to the Texas-activities of [the plaintiff]"); see also Young v. New Haven Advocate, 315 F.3d 256, 263 (4th Cir. 2002) (refusing to exercise jurisdiction over defendants in Virginia where the focus of the defendants' allegedly libelous online articles was Connecticut).

Courts are much more likely to find express aiming when the defendant's online posting focuses on the forum and individuals within the forum. See, e.g., State Farm Fire & Casualty Co. v. Miraglia, 2007 U.S. Dist. LEXIS 75712 (N.D. Tex. Oct. 11, 2007). In Miraglia, the court held that the exercise of personal jurisdiction in Texas was proper on the basis of allegedly defamatory comments about a Texas company that the defendant had posted on an Internet bulletin board operated by Yahoo.com. Id. at *4. According to the court, the defendant's comments were "expressly aimed" at Texas, given that the postings (1) "often referred specifically to . . . Texas locations"; and (2) "specifically named" individuals whom the defendant "knew to be Texas residents." Id.

The fact that Schmidt's posting did not rely on Illinois sources or describe events that occurred in Illinois does not mean that Illinois was any less the "focal point" of her posting. In Zidon v. Pickrell, 344 F. Supp. 2d 624 (D.N.D. 2004), a North Dakota resident brought suit against his former girlfriend, alleging that the ex-girlfriend had defamed him via postings on a website that she had created. Although the website neither drew its content from North Dakota sources nor discussed events that had transpired in North Dakota, the website did contain specific references to the plaintiff's North Dakota residence, the plaintiff's employment in North Dakota, and the plaintiff's family members in North Dakota. On the basis of these facts, the court concluded that the exercise of jurisdiction over the defendant was proper in North Dakota, since the defendant had "particularly and directly targeted North Dakota with her Web site." See Zidon, 344 F. Supp. 2d at 631–32.

Schmidt exhibited a similar intent to "particularly and directly target" Illinois with her posting on lovehimorleavehim.com. Like the postings in Miraglia and Zidon, Schmidt's profile page makes clear that Illinois was the "focal point" of her statements. Schmidt's entire profile page was exclusively concerned with the conduct and reputation of an Illinois resident. See Baird Ex. A. Moreover, Schmidt's profile page mentioned numerous Illinois persons and places in addition to Baird, including the University of Chicago (Baird's employer in Illinois), Baird's wife (a resident of Illinois), and the Latin School (Baird's wife's employer in Illinois). See Baird Ex. A. Schmidt also listed Illinois as one of the relevant locations for her posting, id., and users may search the profile pages on the website by their listed geographic locations, Compl. at ¶ 17. Finally, Schmidt arguably encouraged readers to contact Baird's wife by writing, "I hope someone lets her know about him. . . ." See Baird Ex. A. By making numerous references to Illinois persons and places and by identifying Illinois as one of the profile page's relevant locations, Schmidt did more than target an Illinois resident; she aimed her conduct expressly at Illinois such that Illinois was the focal point of her statements.

C. Schmidt caused foreseeable harm to Baird in Illinois
i. Baird felt the brunt of the harm caused by Schmidt's posting in Illinois

In Illinois, to satisfy the third prong of the effects test, a defendant must cause harm to the plaintiff in Illinois that the defendant knows is likely to be suffered in Illinois. Euromarket, 96 F. Supp. 2d at 835. The court in Jackson found that the brunt of the harm from the allegations of steroid use did not occur in Jackson's home state because he had a national reputation. See 406 F. Supp. 2d at 896. The Jackson court distinguished Calder, noting that "because the entertainment industry of which [Jones] was a part was centered in California, she experienced the most severe harm in California." Id. Other jurisdictions have found that the brunt of the damage done to a plaintiff's personal (as opposed to professional) reputation occurs where she resides. See, e.g., Zidon, 344 F. Supp. 2d at 632.

Baird specifically alleges that Schmidt's actions have caused him harm in Illinois by damaging his reputation, causing emotional distress, and impairing his earning capacity, see Compl. ¶¶ 35–37, allegations that the court will accept as true. Though Baird is seeking jobs nationally, has taken grants from foundations and the federal government, and has traveled frequently for business, Compl. ¶¶ 10–11, Schmidt Aff. ¶ 6, Schmidt will have difficulty convincing the court that Baird has a national reputation analogous to that of Jackson, who was a well-known professional athlete. However, even if the court accepts Schmidt's argument, Baird has nevertheless experienced "the most severe harm" in the forum where he lives and works. Baird's career and marriage are centered in Illinois. See Compl. ¶ 10. Because of the fallout from the posting, his wife forced him to move out of his Illinois home, Compl. ¶ 24, and his Illinois employer suspended him without pay, Compl. ¶ 27. The court will thus likely find that the primary effects of Schmidt's posting were felt in Illinois even if Schmidt's statements did harm Baird's job prospects across the country.

ii. Schmidt should have foreseen that Baird would be harmed in Illinois

Most likely, the court's determination of whether or not Schmidt should have known that Baird was likely to suffer harm in Illinois will closely relate to the extent to which Schmidt expressly aimed her actions at Illinois. In Calder, the Court found that because the libelous story focused on the actress's professional conduct in California, the writer "knew that the brunt of that injury would be felt by [Jones] in the State in which she lives and works...." Calder, 465 U.S. at 784. Similarly, Schmidt knew about, and therefore focused her posting on, Baird's professional and personal misconduct in Illinois. See Baird Ex. A. She also emailed the posting to friends, Schmidt Aff. ¶ 23, increasing the likelihood that someone might contact Baird's wife and employer. Furthermore, upon learning of the posting, Baird alleges that he explicitly asked Schmidt to remove it from the website and she refused. Compl. ¶ 23. At that point, Schmidt could not have doubted the harm that she was causing. Because she knew Baird lived and worked in Illinois, and because she directed her posting at Illinois, she should have foreseen that Baird would likely suffer harm in Illinois.

CONCLUSION

The court will likely find that Schmidt's posting on lovehimorleavehim.com established minimum contacts with Illinois. By intentionally creating an "Illinois-tagged" profile page on a website searchable by geographic location, and by making specific references to several Illinois persons and places throughout her page, Schmidt "expressly aimed" her conduct at Illinois such that Illinois was the "focal point" of her tortious activities. Schmidt's profile page caused Baird to suffer harm in Illinois, and Schmidt knew that the effects of her profile page would be felt primarily in Illinois. Schmidt's posting thus satisfies the criteria for "minimum contacts" under <u>Calder</u> as interpreted by the Seventh Circuit and the Northern District of Illinois.

APPENDIX C

SAMPLE RECORD: *BELL-WESLEY V. O'TOOLE*

SUPERIOR COURT FOR THE STATE OF AMES

REBECCA AND SCOTT BELL-WESLEY,

    Plaintiffs,

v.

DR. STEPHEN O'TOOLE,

    Defendant.

CIVIL ACTION 96–2004

COMPLAINT

JURISDICTION

1. Plaintiffs Rebecca and Scott Bell-Wesley are a married couple residing in the State of Ames.

2. Defendant Stephen O'Toole is a medical doctor who resides and has his medical office in the State of Ames.

CAUSES OF ACTION

3. Plaintiff Scott Bell-Wesley is an architect, under employment of the City of Holmes, City Planning Department.

4. Plaintiff Rebecca Bell-Wesley is an attorney, practicing with the Office of the Attorney General of the State of Ames, in the City of Holmes.

5. Prior to January 4, 2011, Plaintiff Rebecca Bell-Wesley had given birth to three deformed children, each of whom had died within six months after birth. Defendant O'Toole informed Plaintiffs that there was a seventy-five percent chance that any child they conceived would suffer and die from the same congenital deformity.

6. Plaintiffs chose to lead a childless lifestyle by procuring a sterilization operation.

7. On October 16, 2008, Defendant performed a vasectomy on Plaintiff Scott Bell-Wesley for the purpose of preventing conception and birth of a child.

8. Defendant O'Toole was solely responsible for the performance of said operation, and for Plaintiff's post-operative care.

9. Plaintiffs were advised by Defendant that the operation would not render Plaintiff Scott Bell-Wesley sterile immediately, and that an alternative means of birth control should be used by Plaintiffs until ten weeks after the operation.

10. Plaintiffs used an alternate method of birth control for three months after Scott Bell-Wesley's vasectomy.

11. Plaintiffs were further informed by Defendant O'Toole that a sperm count would have to be performed twelve to fourteen weeks after the operation in order to confirm the success of the operation.

12. Plaintiff Scott Bell-Wesley returned to the office of Defendant O'Toole on January 8, 2009, at which time the Defendant performed a sperm count and informed Plaintiffs that Mr. Bell-Wesley was sterile.

13. Defendant O'Toole determined that Plaintiff Rebecca Bell-Wesley was pregnant on April 20, 2010.

14. Plaintiff Rebecca Bell-Wesley gave birth to Frank Michael Bell on January 4, 2011.

15. Plaintiff Scott Bell-Wesley is the biological father of Frank Michael Bell.

16. Defendant's separate acts of negligence were the proximate causes of the injury suffered by Plaintiffs.

17. Plaintiffs were injured by the birth of their unplanned child.

18. Defendant's negligence has denied Plaintiffs their constitutionally protected right of self-determination in matters of childbearing.

19. Plaintiffs have incurred mental, physical, and financial injuries as a result of the conception and birth of their child, for which Defendant is liable.

REMEDY

Wherefore, Plaintiffs pray the Court for the following relief:

20. That Defendant be held liable for the cost of Scott Bell-Wesley's vasectomy, including his medical expenses, his pain and suffering, and Rebecca's loss of consortium during his recuperation period, in the amount of $10,000.

21. That Defendant be held liable for the medical expenses and pain and suffering caused by Rebecca Bell-Wesley's pregnancy and for Scott Bell-Wesley's loss of consortium during the last part of her pregnancy, in the amount of $15,000.

22. That the Defendant be held liable to Plaintiff Rebecca Bell-Wesley for the medical expenses and pain and suffering caused by her giving birth to Frank Michael Bell, in the amount of $25,000.

23. That Defendant be held liable to Plaintiffs for their emotional trauma caused by the conception and birth of an unplanned and unwanted child and for the additional emotional trauma resulting from Plaintiff's reasonable expectation that the child would suffer from a congenital deformity, in the amount of $100,000.

24. That the Defendant be held liable to Plaintiffs for lost earnings incurred as a result of Rebecca Bell-Wesley's pregnancy and the birth and care of their child, in the amount of $16,000.

25. That the Defendant be held liable to Plaintiffs for injury to Plaintiffs' lifestyle, which is impacted financially by the care and rearing of their child, and for their loss of control over their leisure hours, in the amount of $250,000. (See Exhibit A, attached.)

26. That the Defendant be held liable to Plaintiffs for the financial and emotional cost of rearing their child, in the amount of $350,000.

Plaintiffs further pray that the Court order any additional measure of damages as would be just, and that provision for attorney's fees be made.

Respectfully submitted,

Scott and Rebecca Bell-Wesley
by their attorney

Jane E. Harvey

Jane E. Harvey
Llewellyn, Murray & Silber
325 North Bridge Road
Holmes, Ames

Dated: January 16, 2011

EXHIBIT A (in part)

From the 2010 annual report by the Department of Health and Human Services, Washington, D.C.:

The cost of raising a child, outside of possibly purchasing a home, is the single greatest investment a family will make. Current projections, stipulating that there is virtually no limit on what a couple may invest, indicate that the very minimum parents will spend bringing a child up to majority will be $200,000. This figure includes the basic costs of housing, feeding, and clothing the child, as well as the minimum costs of maintaining his/her health up to age eighteen. Addition of even several moderately priced extras—early professional child care, private schooling, college, allowances for serious illness—can push the cost of childrearing beyond $300,000. And these figures do not yet even contemplate the emotional costs of a raising a child.

SUPERIOR COURT FOR THE STATE OF AMES

REBECCA AND SCOTT BELL-WESLEY,

    Plaintiffs,

v.

DR. STEPHEN O'TOOLE,

    Defendant.

CIVIL ACTION 96-2004

DEFENDANT'S ANSWER

1. Defendant admits the allegations in paragraphs 1-5 of Plaintiffs' Complaint.

2. Defendant denies the allegations in paragraph 6 of Plaintiffs' Complaint.

3. Defendant admits the allegations in paragraphs 7-14 of Plaintiffs' Complaint.

4. Defendant is without sufficient information to respond to paragraph 15 of Plaintiffs' Complaint.

5. Defendant denies the allegations in paragraphs 16-26 of Plaintiffs' Complaint.

FIRST AFFIRMATIVE DEFENSE

6. Plaintiffs assumed the risk of possible failure of the sterilization procedure.

7. Since even perfectly performed vasectomies are not successful in all cases, Plaintiffs assumed the risk of failure of the operation, whether resulting from negligence or regrowth.

8. Since the social value of sterilization operations is so high, society has imposed this assumption of risk or waiver of recovery rights for those engaging in a procedure which cannot yet be made 100% effective, regardless of whether negligence was involved.

SECOND AFFIRMATIVE DEFENSE

9. Defendant was not negligent in his operative or post-operative procedures with Plaintiff Scott Bell-Wesley.

10. Plaintiff Scott Bell-Wesley suffered a tubal regrowth which was a statistical failure of the procedure not caused by Defendant's negligence.

THIRD AFFIRMATIVE DEFENSE

11. The birth of a child is always a benefit and a blessing which outweigh any financial costs, as well as any pain and suffering incurred during pregnancy.

12. Where the parents' express purpose in procuring a vasectomy was to prevent the birth of a deformed child, the birth to the parents of a healthy child caused them no injury.

13. Therefore, Plaintiffs did not suffer any damages and Defendant is not liable to Plaintiffs.

FOURTH AFFIRMATIVE DEFENSE

14. Broad social policies prohibit the awarding of child rearing damages in actions for wrongful pregnancy.

15. Therefore, Plaintiffs are not entitled to any damages for the cost of raising their child.

FIFTH AFFIRMATIVE DEFENSE

16. Plaintiffs have failed to mitigate the damages claimed in paragraph 23 of their Complaint by refusing, as they have in the past, to undergo amniocentesis, a safe, simple test conducted early in the pregnancy which would have determined that the child being carried was normal and healthy.

17. Plaintiffs have further failed to mitigate the damages in that they have not offered their unwanted, unplanned child up for adoption.

Respectfully submitted,
Dr. Stephen O'Toole
by their attorney

D. Nathan Neuville

D. Nathan Neuville
Ericson, Swanson and Moses
1977 Pond Ave.
Holmes, Ames

TRIAL RECORD

(Parts have been omitted)

COUNSEL: Mrs. Bell-Wesley, what happened in the months of following the presumably successful sterilization procedure?

REBECCA BELL-WESLEY: Well, shortly after Scott's vasectomy I accepted an offer from the Attorney General to become one of his First Assistant Attorneys General.

COUNSEL: Are there many of these First Assistant Attorneys General?

REBECCA BELL-WESLEY: Oh, no. Just a handful—no more than four or five, each located in a different city in Ames.

COUNSEL: I see, and are you more involved in this new position than in your prior position?

REBECCA BELL-WESLEY: Yes, various department heads reported to me. I also had considerable discretion over the policies promulgated by our office, as well as identification of our litigation goals and authorization of compromises and settlements.

COUNSEL: You say "had." Are you no longer in this position?

REBECCA BELL-WESLEY: It's not clear. I have taken a six-month leave of absence, so I should return to work sometime in May. In the meantime, many things could happen. The Attorney General's Office is a political office, you know.

COUNSEL: Was your position as First Assistant Attorney General obtained by political appointment?

REBECCA BELL-WESLEY: No, the Attorney General usually only bothers himself with hiring or bringing in his own first assistants and department chiefs. I was hired out of law school by a department chief at the time.

COUNSEL: And what was your salary change upon acceptance of your most recent position?

REBECCA BELL-WESLEY: I went from $64,000 per year to $80,000.

SUPERIOR COURT FOR THE STATE OF AMES

REBECCA AND SCOTT BELL-WESLEY,

    Plaintiffs,

v.

DR. STEPHEN O'TOOLE,

    Defendant.

CIVIL ACTION 96-2004

FINDINGS OF FACT AND CONCLUSIONS OF LAW

FINDINGS OF FACT

1. Plaintiffs made a conscious decision to avoid the possibility of the conception and birth of a child. The motive for this decision was their fear of having a deformed child.

2. In furtherance of this decision, Plaintiff Scott Bell-Wesley obtained a vasectomy from Dr. O'Toole on October 16, 2008.

3. Expert testimony showed that Defendant failed to sever properly the tubes of the vas deferens, and the Plaintiff Scott Bell-Wesley was never rendered sterile.

4. Defendant negligently performed a sperm count and informed Plaintiffs that Scott Bell-Wesley had been rendered sterile on January 8, 2009.

5. Defendant is a general practitioner medical doctor who has performed vasectomies in his office over the past few years.

6. Plaintiff Rebecca Bell-Wesley conceived a child and bore that child, Frank Michael Bell, on January 4, 2011.

7. Scott Bell-Wesley has been established as the biological father. The pregnancy and childbirth were normal and without complications, except that they were unplanned; Frank Michael Bell was born healthy and has remained so.

8. Plaintiffs declined to abort the child on moral grounds, and have declined to give the child up for adoption for personal reasons.

9. Plaintiffs' lifestyle has changed dramatically since the birth of the child.

10. Both parents have lost, and will continue to lose, time and wages in their chosen careers as a result of caring for the child.

11. Both parents profess a deep love for their child even though they bring the present action.

12. Expert testimony established that amniocentesis would have revealed that the fetus was not deformed and was in fact in good health.

CONCLUSIONS OF LAW

1. Defendant Dr. Stephen O'Toole negligently performed a vasectomy on Plaintiff Scott Bell-Wesley on October 16, 2008. The vasectomy was unsuccessful.

2. Defendant O'Toole negligently performed a sperm count on January 8, 2009; informed Plaintiffs that the operation was successful; and told them that Scott Bell-Wesley had been rendered sterile.

3. The conception and birth of Plaintiffs' child would not have resulted had the operation been successful.

4. Plaintiffs have stated a cause of action for negligence.

5. Plaintiffs' damages are limited to the out-of-pocket costs, pain and suffering, emotional trauma, lost earnings and loss of consortium associated with Scott Bell-Wesley's vasectomy and Rebecca Bell-Wesley's pregnancy. A reasonable award for these damages is $100,000.

6. Damages are not awardable for the costs associated with rearing a healthy child, because the benefits of a healthy child always outweigh any attendant costs.

DATED: May 13, 2011

Nancy Llewestein
NANCY LLEWESTEIN
Ames Superior Court Judge

SUPERIOR COURT OPINION

Llewenstein, J.

In this bench trial, the Court is faced with a difficult problem involving not only the rights of individuals, but also numerous social and systemic considerations. It is apparent that Scott Bell-Wesley's sterilization operation was performed negligently. Not only was the operation itself ineffective, but also, the Defendant was subsequently negligent in performing a sperm count on Plaintiff Scott Bell-Wesley and in informing the Bell-Wesleys that, on the basis of this test, Mr. Bell-Wesley had been rendered sterile.

Plaintiffs allege that the birth of a healthy son must somehow be compensated by the Defendant. The idea that a child would grow up being supported by someone other than his parents by virtue of the fact that his parents did not plan for or want him is extremely disturbing. The very real inability to assign a dollar amount to such an injury is exceeded only by the harm which such an award could do to families and individuals in our society. Perhaps I am old-fashioned, but I believe people are still filled with mystery, joy and inspiration at the birth of a new human life. In this case, where the Plaintiffs' prior conceptions resulted in the births and tragic deaths of three congenitally deformed infants, the birth to them of a healthy child is truly a blessing. The benefits of a healthy child clearly outweigh any and all costs associated with raising the child.

Scott Bell-Wesley's vasectomy was improperly performed and the post-operative care he received was inadequate. The Defendant is liable for his improper medical treatment, and therefore, damages of $100,000 are awarded to Plaintiffs. However, Ames will not join the ranks of jurisdictions recognizing child-rearing costs as an element of damages in a wrongful pregnancy action. The benefits of a healthy child always outweigh any attendant costs or burdens. This case is no different.

SUPERIOR COURT FOR THE STATE OF AMES

REBECCA AND SCOTT BELL-WESLEY,

    Plaintiffs,

v.

DR. STEPHEN O'TOOLE,

    Defendant.

CIVIL ACTION 96-2004

JUDGMENT

JUDGMENT OF TRIAL COURT

The issues in the above action having duly been heard by this Court, and this Court having made and filed its findings of fact and conclusions of law on May 13, 2011, it is, therefore,

ORDERED, ADJUDGED, AND DECREED, that judgment be entered for Plaintiffs as to Defendant's acts of negligence and Plaintiffs be awarded $100,000 in damages.

DATED: May 20, 2011

                                      John James
                                   Clerk of Court

SUPERIOR COURT FOR THE STATE OF AMES

REBECCA AND SCOTT BELL-WESLEY,
 	
    Plaintiffs,
 	
    v.
 	
DR. STEPHEN O'TOOLE,
 	
    Defendant.
	CIVIL ACTION 96-2004
	
	NOTICE OF APPEAL

Notice is hereby given that Petitioners, Rebecca and Scott Bell-Wesley, appeal to the Court of Appeals for the State of Ames (N.E. Division), from the final judgment entered in this action on the 20th day of May, 2011.

Dated: May 21, 2011

                                                  Jane E. Harvey
                                                  Jane E. Harvey
                                                  Attorney for Appellants
                                                  Llewellyn, Murray & Silber
                                                  325 North Bridge Road
                                                  Holmes, Ames

SUPERIOR COURT FOR THE STATE OF AMES

REBECCA AND SCOTT BELL-WESLEY,

    Plaintiffs,

v.

DR. STEPHEN O'TOOLE,

    Defendant.

CIVIL ACTION 96-2004

STIPULATION OF THE RECORD

It is hereby stipulated by the attorneys for the respective parties in the above-named action, that the following shall constitute the transcript of the record on appeal.

1. Pleadings before the Superior Court of the State of Ames:

    a. Summons (omitted)

    b. Complaint

    c. Exhibit A

    d. Return of Service (omitted)

    e. Answer

    f. Affidavit of Service (omitted)

2. Trial Record

3. Findings of Fact and Conclusions of Law

4. Opinion of the Superior Court of the State of Ames

5. Judgment of the Superior Court of the State of Ames

6. Notice of Appeal

7. This Designation

COURT OF APPEALS FOR THE STATE OF AMES
(N.E. DIVISION)

REBECCA AND SCOTT BELL-WESLEY,

    Plaintiffs,

DR. STEPHEN O'TOOLE,

    Defendant.

Sitting Below:
Judge Llewenstein
CIVIL ACTION 96-2004

OPINION AFFIRMING THE TRIAL COURT'S DECISIONS OF LAW

Syllabus: This case arises out of facts centering around the birth of a child. . . .

    . . . .

The Plaintiffs' appeal in this case must be rejected by this Court. We do so largely on the same grounds that led Judge Llewenstein to reject them in the first instance. While we will explain ourselves at length below, we do not wish to imply that our discussion intimates anything but agreement with Judge Llewenstein's views. . . .

COURT OF APPEALS FOR THE STATE OF AMES
(N.E. DIVISION)

REBECCA AND SCOTT BELL-WESLEY,

    Plaintiffs,

CIVIL ACTION 96-2004

NOTICE OF APPEAL

DR. STEPHEN O'TOOLE,

    Defendant.

Notice is hereby given that Petitioners, Rebecca and Scott Bell-Wesley, petition for certiorari the Supreme Court of the State of Ames, from the decision of the Court of Appeals for the State of Ames (N.E. Division) in this action on the 13th day of July, 2011.

Dated: July 21, 2011   *Jane E. Harvey*

                                           Jane E. Harvey
                                           Attorney for Appellants
                                           Llewellyn, Murray & Silber
                                           325 North Bridge Road
                                           Holmes, Ames

IN THE AMES SUPREME COURT

REBECCA AND SCOTT BELL-WESLEY,

    Petitioners,

v.

DR. STEPHEN O'TOOLE,

    Respondent.

Sitting Below:

Judge Trimble

Judge Lule

Judge Haentgens
CIVIL ACTION 96-2004

GRANT OF CERTIORARI

This Court hereby grants certiorari on the following issue in the case of Bell-Wesley v. O'Toole:

Whether the cost of raising a healthy child should properly be included as an element of damages in a wrongful pregnancy action.

Assume that no arguable issue exists concerning:

1. Plaintiffs' timeliness in bringing the action under the relevant statute of limitations.

2. Defendant's negligence in performing the operation and in performing the sperm count upon which he relied in informing Plaintiffs that Scott Bell-Wesley was sterile.

3. The actual <u>amount</u> of damages as a goal upon appeal. Quantification and award of each element is determined upon remand; the issue then is whether the court should recognize each type of damage as recoverable.

20

APPENDIX D

SAMPLE APPELLANT BRIEF: *BELL-WESLEY V. O'TOOLE*

IN THE SUPREME COURT OF THE
STATE OF AMES

CIVIL ACTION NO. 96-2004

SCOTT AND REBECCA BELL-WESLEY, PLAINTIFFS-APPELLANTS

V.

STEPHEN O'TOOLE, DEFENDANT-APPELLEE

BRIEF FOR THE PLAINTIFFS-APPELLANTS

> Jane E. Harvey
> Attorney for the Plaintiffs-Appellants
> Llewellyn, Murray & Silber
> 325 North Bridge Road
> Holmes, Ames

TABLE OF CONTENTS

TABLE OF CONTENTS i

TABLE OF AUTHORITIES ii

PRELIMINARY STATEMENT 1

QUESTION PRESENTED 1

STATEMENT OF FACTS 2

SUMMARY OF THE ARGUMENT 4

ARGUMENT 5

I. STANDARD OF REVIEW 5

II. THE SUPERIOR COURT ERRED BY REFUSING TO FULLY COMPENSATE THE BELL-WESLEYS FOR ALL FORESEEABLE DAMAGES RESULTING FROM SCOTT'S NEGLIGENT STERILIZATION, INCLUDING THE COSTS OF HAVING AND RAISING THEIR CHILD 5

    A. The Bell-Wesleys Should Recover Damages for All of Their Injuries, Including the Costs of Raising Their Son, Because Such Damages Are Reasonable and Foreseeable, and Thus Subject to Recovery Under Standard Tort Law Principles. 5

    B. Policy Considerations Require that Injuries to Scott and Rebecca be Compensated Fully Like those in any Other Negligence Case. 7

III. ALTERNATIVELY, IF THIS COURT WILL NOT AWARD FULL DAMAGES, THIS COURT SHOULD AWARD DAMAGES FOR THE COSTS OF RAISING FRANK BELL-WESLEY OFFSET BY THE BENEFIT OF HAVING HIM 10

CONCLUSION 11

TABLE OF AUTHORITIES

CASES   **Page(s)**

Burke v. Rivo,
551 N.E.2d 1 (Mass. 1990) 7, 9, 10, 11

Custodio v. Bauer,
59 Cal. Rptr. 463 (Cal Ct. App. 1967) 6

Kingsbury v. Smith,
442 A.2d 1003 (N.H. 1982) 8

Lovelace Med. Ctr. v. Mendez,
805 P.2d 603 (N.M. 1991) 5, 6, 8

Marciniak v. Lundborg,
450 N.W.2d 243 (Wis. 1989) 5, 6, 9

Ochs v. Borrelli,
445 A.2d 883 (Conn. 1982) 10

Provencio v. Wenrich,
261 P.3d 1089 (N.M. 2011) 7

Sherlock v. Stillwater Clinic,
260 N.W.2d 169 (Minn. 1977) 10, 11

Univ. of Ariz. Health Sciences Ctr. v. Sup. Ct.,
667 P.2d 1294 (Ariz. 1983) 10

Zehr v. Haugen,
871 P.2d 1006 (Or. 1994) 6, 9

OTHER AUTHORITIES

Michael T. Murtaugh, Wrongful Birth: The Courts' Dilemma in Determining a Remedy for a Blessed Event, 27 Pace L. Rev. 241 (2007) 7

Restatement (Second) of Torts 10

W. Page Keeton et al., Prosser and Keeton on the Law of Torts (5th ed. 1984) 5

PRELIMINARY STATEMENT

Following Stephen O'Toole's negligent performance of a vasectomy on Scott Bell-Wesley, Scott and his wife, Rebecca, conceived and gave birth to their son, Frank. The Bell-Wesleys sued O'Toole in the Superior Court for the State of Ames, seeking damages for his negligence, which resulted in their unplanned pregnancy and the unexpected birth of their son. R. at 1-2. Following a bench trial, the Superior Court determined that O'Toole had acted negligently when he botched Mr. Bell-Wesley's vasectomy and follow-up testing, and the court awarded the Bell-Wesleys damages to compensate them for their medical expenses, pain and suffering, and loss of consortium. R. at 12-15. Notwithstanding this finding of negligence, the Superior Court declined to award the Bell-Wesleys all reasonable and foreseeable damages stemming from the vasectomy that O'Toole negligently performed. Specifically, the Court refused to compensate the Bell-Wesleys for the financial burden associated with raising their son. R. at 14. The Bell-Wesleys appealed the Superior Court's denial of full damages to the Court of Appeals for the State of Ames, R. at 16, and the Court of Appeals also declined to require that O'Toole pay full damages, including the reasonable costs of their son's upbringing, R. at 18. The Bell-Wesleys petitioned this Court for further review. R. at 19. This Court granted *certiorari* to determine whether the Bell-Wesleys can recover the costs of raising their son to majority. R. at 20.

QUESTION PRESENTED

O'Toole negligently performed a vasectomy and follow-up testing on Scott Bell-Wesley. As a result of O'Toole's negligence, the Bell-Wesleys unexpectedly conceived and gave birth to a son, incurring the costs of his delivery and upbringing. Under fundamental tort law principles, individuals are liable for all injuries flowing naturally and foreseeably from their negligence. Should O'Toole be held liable for the full results of his negligence, including the extensive costs associated with raising a child?

STATEMENT OF FACTS

Scott Bell-Wesley is an architect with the Holmes City Planning Department, and his wife, Rebecca, is an attorney in the Attorney General's Office of the State of Ames. R. at 1, 9. The Bell-Wesleys made a conscious decision to forego having children. R. at 1. They made this difficult decision after they previously had given birth to three children, all of whom tragically died within six months of birth due to a genetic congenital disorder. Id. Their doctor, Defendant-Appellee Stephen O'Toole, advised the Bell-Wesleys that there was a seventy-five percent chance that any future child they conceived would suffer from the same lethal congenital disorder. Id. Based on O'Toole's advice and their fear of bringing another ill child into the world, the Bell-Wesleys chose to remain childless. R. at 1, 11. They did not adopt. See id. Instead, they devoted their lives to each other and to their careers. See R. at 3, 9.

In order to guarantee the lifestyle they had chosen and to guard against the risk of delivering a fourth sick child, the Bell-Wesleys asked O'Toole to perform a vasectomy on Scott on October 16, 2008. R. at 1. O'Toole botched the procedure and failed to sever the tubes of Scott's vas deferens properly, leaving Scott capable of fathering another child. R. at 11. O'Toole then compounded his surgical error by improperly testing Scott Bell-Wesley's sperm count. Id. Based on the results of this test, O'Toole informed the Bell-Wesley family that he had successfully sterilized Scott. R. at 2, 11. O'Toole was incorrect, and the Bell-Wesleys remained unaware that Scott was still fertile. R. at 2, 11.

Shortly after Scott's vasectomy in 2008, and based on the choices she and Scott had made about their lifestyle, Rebecca accepted a promotion to First Assistant Attorney General of the State of Ames. R. at 9. Her salary increased from $64,000 to $80,000 per year. R. at 10. The Bell-Wesleys also resumed marital relations after O'Toole informed them that the vasectomy had been a success. R. at 2.

In April 2010, Rebecca and Scott Bell-Wesley discovered that they were pregnant again. R. at 2. Even though the Bell-Wesleys feared that their unborn child would suffer the same fate as their three deceased children, they decided not to terminate the pregnancy on moral grounds. R. at 11-12. They also decided not to undergo amniocentesis, which the Court concluded would have revealed that the Bell-Wesleys' son was healthy. R. at 12. On January 4, 2011, Rebecca gave birth to a healthy baby boy, Frank Michael. R. at 2.

The Superior Court found that O'Toole was negligent. R. at 12. The court determined that he negligently performed Scott's vasectomy and negligently performed a sperm count test on Scott, leaving the Bell-Wesleys unaware that they could conceive a child. Id. The court further determined that the Bell-Wesleys' child would not have been born but for O'Toole's negligent treatment of Scott Bell-Wesley. Id. As a result of O'Toole's negligent acts, the Court held that he was liable to the Bell-Wesley family and ordered him to pay $100,000 to cover the Bell-Wesleys' out-of-pocket medical costs, pain and suffering, lost earnings, and loss of consortium. R. at 13. None of these decisions are challenged on appeal.

The Superior Court, however, decided not to award the Bell-Wesleys damages for the costs associated with raising their son to adulthood. While the Bell-Wesleys obviously love their son deeply, R. at 12, his conception and birth have nonetheless caused them severe emotional, physical, and financial harm, R. at 2. Their son's unexpected birth has forced the Bell-Wesleys to alter their lives dramatically. R. at 12. Both parents have lost, and continue to lose, time and wages from their careers in order to care for their child. Id. Rebecca's leave of absence in connection with the pregnancy has also jeopardized her job. R. at 8. The financial and emotional costs of raising Frank present the Bell-Wesleys with a formidable burden. In fact, the record shows that the very minimum that most parents will spend to raise a child is $200,000. R. at 5. Even though the Court found that "Scott Bell-Wesley's vasectomy was improperly performed and the postoperative care he received was inadequate," the Court refused to compensate the Bell-Wesleys for the extensive financial costs associated with raising their son. R. at 14. The Bell-Wesleys appeal this decision. R. at 16, 19.

SUMMARY OF THE ARGUMENT

The fundamental tort goals of deterrence and fairness require that O'Toole pay for the reasonably foreseeable damages he caused when he negligently performed Scott Bell-Wesley's vasectomy and subsequent sperm count. This Court should seek to place the Bell-Wesleys in the same position they would have been in had O'Toole performed Scott Bell-Wesley's vasectomy or follow-up testing correctly. Their damage award should reflect the pain and suffering, emotional trauma, lost earnings, costs of raising their son, Frank, and the sacrifice of their chosen lifestyle. The trial court's insistence that a child's birth is always a costless blessing is without merit or any factual basis and disregards the purpose and structure of tort law.

Should this Court not award the Bell-Wesleys full damages for policy reasons, this Court should nevertheless apply an alternative rule adopted by some jurisdictions and award damages for the costs of raising Frank offset by the benefit of having him. Although the emotional benefits the Bell-Wesleys receive from parenthood are of an entirely different kind than the financial injuries and pain and suffering inflicted on them by O'Toole's negligence, this rule presents the most just and reasonable alternative to full compensation.

ARGUMENT

I. STANDARD OF REVIEW

Whether the Bell-Wesley family can recover the full cost of raising a healthy child as an element of damages in a wrongful pregnancy action is a question of law and is thus reviewed *de novo*. See Lovelace Med. Ctr. v. Mendez, 805 P.2d 603, 614 (N.M. 1991).

II. THE SUPERIOR COURT ERRED BY REFUSING TO FULLY COMPENSATE THE BELL-WESLEYS FOR ALL FORESEEABLE DAMAGES RESULTING FROM SCOTT'S NEGLIGENT STERILIZATION, INCLUDING THE COSTS OF HAVING AND RAISING THEIR CHILD.

A. The Bell-Wesleys Should Recover Damages for All of Their Injuries, Including the Costs of Raising Their Son, Because Such Damages Are Reasonable and Foreseeable and Thus Subject to Recovery Under Standard Tort Law Principles.

This Court should overturn the denial of the Bell-Wesleys' claim for compensation for the expense of raising their unplanned child because the Superior Court's refusal to award plaintiffs all foreseeable damages—as is the standard in tort cases—was erroneous. The general rule in tort cases is that "a person has an obligation to exercise reasonable care so as to not cause foreseeable harm to another." Marciniak v. Lundborg, 450 N.W.2d 243, 245 (Wis. 1989) (citation omitted) (holding that costs of raising child to majority may be recovered by parents as damages for negligently performed sterilization procedure). Under this rule, individuals are held liable for all injuries flowing naturally and foreseeably from their negligence. See W. Page Keeton et al., Prosser and Keeton on the Law of Torts 43 (5th ed. 1984) (describing theories of liability for negligence). This rule applies equally to tort cases such as these—so-called wrongful pregnancy or wrongful conception cases. As one court explained, "[w]here the purpose of the physician's actions is to prevent conception through sterilization, and the physician's actions are performed negligently, traditional principles of tort law require that the physician be held legally responsible for the consequences which have in fact occurred."

Marciniak, 450 N.W.2d at 248. Here, the Superior Court found that O'Toole was negligent when he botched Scott Bell-Wesley's vasectomy and follow-up sperm count. R. at 12. The Superior Court also concluded that O'Toole's failed procedure resulted in the birth of the Bell-Wesleys' son. Id. None of these factual findings are challenged on appeal. Accordingly, under the basic rules governing damages in torts cases, included cases such as these, the Superior Court should have awarded the Bell-Wesleys all foreseeable damages associated with Frank's birth. The Superior Court, in contravention of the standard rules governing tort cases, failed to do so when it declined to award the Bell-Wesley family *all* reasonably foreseeable damages resulting from O'Toole's negligence, and this decision was legal error.

The Superior Court should have awarded the Bell-Wesleys damages that included the costs of raising Frank Bell-Wesley to majority, because such damages are "foreseeable." In wrongful pregnancy cases, courts have determined that foreseeable damages include the costs of having and raising an unexpected child. Marciniak, 450 N.W.2d at 248. This is because the obvious consequences of a botched vasectomy include the conception and birth of an unplanned child and the associated costs of raising that child. See id. at 245 ("We therefore conclude that the parents of a healthy child may recover the costs of raising the child from a physician who negligently performs a sterilization."); Custodio v. Bauer, 59 Cal. Rptr. 463, 476 (Cal Ct. App. 1967) (noting that recoverable damages included the cost of the unsuccessful operation, mental, physical and nervous pain and suffering during pregnancy, and costs of rearing the child); Zehr v. Haugen, 871 P.2d 1006, 1011-13 (Or. 1994) (commenting that "expenses of raising the child and providing for the child's college education" are recoverable in cases "based on defendant physician's alleged failure to perform a tubal ligation"); Lovelace, 805 P.2d at 612 (recognizing that doctor who performed negligent sterilization can be required to pay "damages in the form of the reasonable expenses to raise [later born child] to majority"); Provencio v. Wenrich, 261 P.3d 1089 (N.M. 2011) (to similar effect); see also Michael T. Murtaugh, Wrongful Birth: The Courts' Dilemma in Determining a Remedy for a Blessed Event, 27 Pace L. Rev. 241, 300–03 (2007) (arguing that courts should focus on the intent of the plaintiffs in undergoing a vasectomy, and should award costs for rearing a child to those motivated by non-economic reasons).

Just like the plaintiffs in Marciniak, Custodio, Zehr, Lovelace, and Provencio, the Bell-Wesleys have sustained serious physical, financial, and emotional injuries as a result of O'Toole's negligent sterilization and follow-up testing, and they are entitled to recover all foreseeable damages, including the cost of raising Frank. The Superior Court's failure to award damages for child-raising has left the couple uncompensated for significant economic harms, namely the estimated $200,000 it will cost to raise Frank to majority. See R. at 5. The costs of raising Frank are a direct financial injury to the parents, no different in immediate effect than the medical expenses resulting from the wrongful conception and birth of a child. Therefore, under the normal rules of damages in tort cases, which require that plaintiffs receive *all* foreseeable damages, the Bell-Wesleys should recover for the costs of rearing Frank.

    B. Policy Considerations Require that Injuries to Scott and Rebecca be Compensated Fully Like those in any Other Negligence Case.

The Superior Court erred in rejecting the Bell-Wesleys' claim for child rearing damages as a matter of public policy, because public policy counsels that the Court should allow plaintiffs to recover full damages that reasonably flow from negligent sterilization procedures, including the cost of child care. Where a couple elects not to have children, it should be presumed as a matter of policy that the birth of a child would not benefit them. See Burke v. Rivo, 551 N.E.2d 1, 4 (Mass. 1990). As the Burke court explained, "[t]he very fact that a person has sought medical intervention to prevent him or her from having a child demonstrates that, for that person, the benefits of parenthood did not outweigh the burdens, economic and otherwise, of having a child." Id.; see also Lovelace, 805 P.2d at 612-13 ("an interest to be protected in this setting is the parents' desire to safeguard the financial security of their family").

Although the Bell-Wesleys love their son greatly, Frank's conception and birth substantially injured the Bell-Wesleys' physical, emotional, and financial well-being. The couple's decision to undergo a vasectomy demonstrated that they rejected any benefits of procreation. The Bell-Wesleys assessed their opportunities and resources and radically altered the goals of their marriage. They decided to devote more time to each other and their careers, only to have their expectations shattered as a result of O'Toole's negligence. While they could have adopted children, the Bell-Wesleys instead chose to pursue a childless lifestyle, recognizing that parenthood entails numerous costs, burdens, and responsibilities that may outweigh its attendant joys. Here, however, the Court substituted its own value judgment for that of the Bell-Wesleys and ignored the legitimate economic damages suffered by the Bell-Wesleys that are routinely recognized by the law of torts and courts in several other jurisdictions.

Furthermore, the Superior Court's decision not to award full damages to the Bell-Wesleys contravenes the fundamental tort law policy in favor of fully deterring negligent behavior. Full recovery by wrongful pregnancy claimants is necessary to deter negligence in performing vasectomies and post-operative care. See Kingsbury v. Smith, 442 A.2d 1003, 1005 (N.H. 1982) (stating that failure to recognize wrongful birth claims would lower the standard of professional conduct and expertise in the area of family planning). Faced with a blameworthy defendant, O'Toole, and his innocent victims, the Bell-Wesleys, this Court does society a disservice by granting immunity to the tortfeasor and leaving his victims uncompensated.

Negligent physicians like O'Toole must not be allowed to escape the consequences of their carelessness. Thus, courts must assess doctors for the full costs of their malfeasance in order to provide adequate incentives for safe, effective medical procedures.

In addition, recognition of the Bell-Wesleys' claim will not result in psychological harm to Frank if he discovers that he was unplanned. The public record of this case is already replete with references to Frank being unplanned—a fact that will not change depending on what damages are awarded. Furthermore, even if damages make a difference, Frank could easily be protected from this unlikely event by keeping the names of those involved in this action confidential. If anything, Frank's psychological well-being dictates a full recovery because any recovery by the Bell-Wesleys will inure to Frank's emotional benefit. It will relieve the economic pressure of raising an unexpected child and permit the parents to concentrate on giving the child the love and care he needs. See, e.g., Burke, 551 N.E.2d at 4-5; Marciniak, 450 N.W.2d at 246 ("We do not perceive that the [plaintiffs] in bringing this suit are in any way disparaging the value of their child's life. They are, to the contrary, attempting to enhance it"). Accordingly, concern for Frank's psychological harm does not support denying the Bell-Wesleys full compensation.

Nor, as argued by O'Toole below, are damages too speculative in this case. Childrearing costs can be estimated satisfactorily using data available from the government and other sources, see R. at 5, and Courts have previously accepted these estimates. See Marciniak, 450 N.W.2d at 247 (noting in negligent sterilization case, "[j]uries are frequently called on to answer damage questions that are far less predictable than those presented here"); see also Zehr, 871 P.2d at 1012 (holding that damages for child rearing are "not, as a matter of law, too speculative to permit recovery").

Accordingly, this Court should award the Bell-Wesleys damages for all of their injuries, including the costs of raising their son.

III. ALTERNATIVELY, IF THIS COURT WILL NOT AWARD FULL DAMAGES, IT SHOULD AWARD DAMAGES FOR THE COSTS OF RAISING FRANK BELL-WESLEY OFFSET BY THE BENEFIT OF HAVING HIM.

If this Court is unwilling to award full damages, the Court should alternatively award damages to the Bell-Wesleys for the costs of raising their son, offset by the benefits the Bell-Wesleys derive from having a son. This rule is consistent with the tort law's goals of deterrence and fair compensation for injuries, and it has been applied by a number of jurisdictions to avoid a situation where a plaintiff is unable to recover the costs associated with caring for a child born as a result of a negligent sterilization procedure. See, e.g., Univ. of Ariz. Health Sciences Ctr. v. Sup. Ct., 667 P.2d 1294, 1299 (Ariz. 1983); Ochs v. Borrelli, 445 A.2d 883, 886 (Conn. 1982); Sherlock v. Stillwater Clinic, 260 N.W.2d 169, 175–76 (Minn. 1977). The rule requires the court to subtract the estimated benefit of the child to the parents from their recovery. See, e.g., Burke, 551 N.E.2d at 5. This approach also conforms with the Restatement (Second) of Torts, which states:

> When the defendant's tortious conduct has caused harm to the plaintiff or to his property and in so doing has conferred a special benefit to the interest of the plaintiff that was harmed, the value of the benefit conferred is considered in mitigation of damages, to the extent that this is equitable.

§ 920 (1979); see also Ochs, 445 A.2d at 886 (citing the Restatement to this effect).

In a similar failed vasectomy case, the Minnesota Supreme Court ruled that a husband and wife were entitled to recovery for the costs of raising an unwanted child minus "the value of the child's aid, comfort, and society." Sherlock, 260 N.W.2d at 176. Similarly, the Massachusetts Supreme Judicial Court ruled that a woman could recover for the costs of raising a healthy but unwanted child, offset by the estimated benefit of the child, after a doctor negligently performed a sterilization procedure. Burke, 551 N.E.2d at 6. While that court's ruling was limited to those failed sterilizations that were originally obtained for financial or economic reasons, the important policy considerations underlying the court's ruling also apply to situations in which a sterilization is obtained for non-economic reasons and the family makes substantial financial decisions based on that choice.

Cases like Sherlock and Burke are analogous to the situation here, where an unplanned birth resulted from a botched sterilization procedure. Applying the same reasoning here, this Court could credit any benefits of having a child against the Bell-Wesley family's substantial financial loss when determining appropriate damages. Although the emotional benefits the Bell-Wesleys receive through the joys of parenthood are of an entirely different nature and kind than the financial injuries and the pain and suffering inflicted on them by O'Toole's negligence, this rule has the advantage of providing something closer to full and fair remuneration to the plaintiffs. This is essential because the Bell-Wesleys' deep love for their son does not negate the fact that his birth was unplanned. The Bell-Wesleys' affection for Frank will not provide them with the resources to cover his expenses, nor will it replace the time and energy diverted from their careers. Therefore, in the event that this Court finds the birth of an unwanted child after a negligent sterilization a benefit, it should apply the offset rule from Sherlock and Burke, and remand this case for a determination of the costs shouldered by the Bell-Wesleys as a result of raising their son and the benefits derived from his birth.

CONCLUSION

O'Toole's repeated negligence caused the Bell-Wesleys substantial physical, financial, and emotional injuries that were left uncompensated by the Superior Court. Therefore, this Court should reverse the judgment of the Superior Court and Court of Appeals of the State of Ames and award full recovery to the Bell-Wesleys.

Respectfully Submitted,

Jane E. Harvey

Jane E. Harvey
Attorney for the Plaintiffs-Appellants

APPENDIX E

SAMPLE APPELLEE BRIEF: *BELL-WESLEY V. O'TOOLE*

IN THE SUPREME COURT OF THE
STATE OF AMES

CIVIL ACTION NO. 96-2004

SCOTT AND REBECCA BELL-WESLEY, PLAINTIFFS-APPELLANTS

V.

STEPHEN O'TOOLE, DEFENDANT-APPELLEE

BRIEF FOR THE DEFENDANT-APPELLEE

> D. Nathan Neuville
> Attorney for the Defendant-Appellee
> Ericson, Swanson and Moses
> 1977 Yvonne Ave.
> Smith, Ames

TABLE OF CONTENTS

TABLE OF CONTENTS i

TABLE OF AUTHORITIES ii

PRELIMINARY STATEMENT 1

QUESTION PRESENTED 1

STATEMENT OF THE FACTS 1

SUMMARY OF THE ARGUMENT 3

STANDARD OF REVIEW 3

ARGUMENT 4

I. THE COURT SHOULD NOT AWARD THE APPELLANTS DAMAGES FOR THE COSTS OF RAISING THEIR NORMAL, HEALTHY SON TO MAJORITY 4

A. Frank's Birth Did Not Injure the Appellants Because Giving Birth to a Healthy Child Cannot be an "Injury" 4

B. Even if the Birth of Appellants' Son Constitutes an "Injury," Frank's Birth Did Not Cause A Compensable Economic Injury to the Bell-Wesleys Because They Sought Sterilization for Purely Non-Economic Reasons 7

II. THIS COURT SHOULD NOT ADOPT A RULE THAT OFFSETS THE APPELLANTS' DAMAGES BY THE BENEFITS OF A CHILD BECAUSE SUCH BENEFITS CANNOT BE QUANTIFIED 8

III. EVEN IF THE APPELLANTS' OFFSET RULE APPLIES, THE EMOTIONAL BENEFITS THE BELL-WESLEYS WILL RECEIVE FROM THEIR SON OUTWEIGH THEIR FINANCIAL COSTS 9

CONCLUSION 10

TABLE OF AUTHORITIES

CASES   Page(s)

Boone v. Mullendore,
416 So.2d 718 (Ala. 1982) 5, 8

Burke v. Rivo,
551 N.E.2d 1 (Mass. 1990) 7

Chaffee v. Seslar,
786 N.E.2d 705 (Ind. 2003) 4, 8

Cockrum v. Baumgartner,
447 N.E.2d 385 (Ill. 1983) 8

Girdley v. Coats,
825 S.W.2d 295 (Mo. 1992) 5, 6

Hartke v. McKelway,
526 F. Supp. 97 (D.D.C. 1981), aff'd 707 F.2d 1544 (D.C. Cir. 1983), cert. denied
464 U.S. 983 (1983) 7

Hitzemann v. Adam,
518 N.W.2d 102 (Neb. 1994) 5, 6

McKernan v. Aasheim,
687 P.2d 850 (Wash. 1984) 5, 6

Ochs v. Borelli,
445 A.2d 883 (Conn. 1982) 8

Pub. Health Trust v. Brown,
388 So.2d 1084 (Fla. App. 1980) 9

Rieck v. Medical Protective Co.,
219 N.W.2d 242 (Wis. 1974) 5, 6

Sherlock v. Stillwater Clinic,
260 N.W.2d 169 (Minn. 1977) 3, 9

Terrell v. Garcia,
496 S.W.2d 124 (Texas Civ. App. 1973) 5, 8

Univ. of Ariz. Health Sciences Ctr. v. Sup. Ct.,
667 P.2d 1294 (Ariz. 1983) 9

OTHER AUTHORITIES

Judy S. Loitherstein, <u>Towards Full Recovery—The Future of Damages Awards in Wrongful Pregnancy Cases</u>, 25 Suffolk U. L. Rev. 735 (1991) 4

PRELIMINARY STATEMENT

Appellants Rebecca and Scott Bell-Wesley brought suit in the Superior Court of the State of Ames against Dr. Stephen O'Toole, an established Ames physician, seeking damages for the birth of a healthy, normal child following an unsuccessful sterilization. R. at 1–4. The Appellants sought at trial to obtain approximately $766,000 in damages, including $250,000 for injury to their lifestyle and $350,000 for the financial and emotional costs of raising their son Frank. R. at 3. The Superior Court found that Mr. Bell-Wesley's vasectomy, which was performed by Dr. O'Toole, was unsuccessful. R. at 11, 12. As a result, the Superior Court awarded the Bell-Wesleys damages for their out-of-pocket costs, pain and suffering, and loss of consortium incident to the vasectomy. R. at 13. The Superior Court refused to award the Bell-Wesleys damages for the costs of raising their son, holding that the benefits they received from their healthy, normal child obviously outweighed the costs of rearing him. R. at 14. The Court of Appeals for the State of Ames affirmed. R. at 18. The Bell-Wesleys now appeal the lower courts' decisions.

QUESTION PRESENTED

Plaintiff-Appellants Rebecca and Scott Bell-Wesley sought sterilization for non-economic reasons. After performing an unsuccessful vasectomy, Defendant-Appellee Dr. Stephen O'Toole mistakenly informed Scott Bell-Wesley he was sterile. Appellants thereafter conceived and gave birth to a healthy, normal son, Frank. Should the Appellants' damages be limited to the costs associated with the sterilization procedure and pregnancy?

STATEMENT OF THE FACTS

The Appellants are a successful professional couple residing in Holmes, Ames. R. at 1. Scott Bell-Wesley is an architect and Rebecca Bell-Wesley is an Assistant Attorney General for the State of Ames. R. at 1. On three occasions before the January 2011 birth of their son, the Appellants attempted to start a family. R. at 1. Each time, however, Ms. Bell-Wesley gave birth to a sick infant that died within six months due to a fatal congenital abnormality. R. at 1. Dr. O'Toole accurately informed the Appellants that there was a seventy-five percent chance that any child they conceived would suffer from the same abnormality. R. at 1. For the sole purpose of avoiding the conception of another sick child, the Appellants decided to have Mr. Bell-Wesley sterilized. R. at 7.

On October 16, 2008, Dr. O'Toole performed a vasectomy on Mr. Bell-Wesley. R. at 1, 11. The surgery was not successful. R. at 1–2. After a follow-up sperm count test, Dr. O'Toole mistakenly informed Mr. Bell-Wesley that he was sterile. R. at 2. Eighteen months after the vasectomy, Ms. Bell-Wesley discovered that she was pregnant. R. at 2. On January 4, 2011, the Bell-Wesleys gave birth to a healthy, normal son, Frank. R. at 11–12. The Appellants have continued to raise Frank and have declined to put him up for adoption. R. at 12.

On January 16, 2011, the Bell-Wesleys filed suit against Dr. O'Toole. R. at 2. After a bench trial, the Superior Court held Dr. O'Toole liable and awarded the Bell-Wesleys $100,000 for their out-of-pocket costs, pain and suffering, and loss of consortium. R. at 13. The Court, however, declined to award the $350,000 in damages that the Bell-Wesleys sought to compensate them for raising a normal, healthy son because the Bell-Wesleys, who for many years tried to have a child, obviously benefitted from their son's birth. R. at 14. Dissatisfied with the amount of damages they had been awarded, the Bell-Wesleys appealed. R. at 16. The Court of Appeals affirmed the Superior Court's decision, agreeing that the Bell-Wesleys could not recover damages relating to child-rearing costs because the benefits of a having a healthy child obviously outweigh any supposed burdens. R. at 18. Seeking a different result, the Bell-Wesleys appealed the decision to this Court. R. at 19.

SUMMARY OF THE ARGUMENT

This Court should affirm both lower courts' decisions that the Appellants' damages are limited to the out-of-pocket costs, pain and suffering, and loss of consortium incident to the vasectomy. Their damages should not include the costs of raising their healthy, normal son to majority. The Appellants sought sterilization for non-economic reasons. Therefore, they have not sustained an injury from Frank's birth. Moreover, awarding the full costs of raising Frank to majority will harm his mental health, discourage doctors from performing needed sterilizations, and grant a windfall to the Appellants.

This Court should also decline to adopt a rule that would offset the Appellants' claimed damages by the benefits of having a healthy son because courts cannot, and should not, quantify the benefits of a child. Attempting to monetize the benefit enjoyed by the Appellants in Frank's existence demeans his life. However, even if this Court adopts this alternative rule, the emotional benefits the Appellants will receive from Frank far outweigh the costs associated with his parenting.

STANDARD OF REVIEW

While this court reviews issues of law *de novo*, it must defer to the trial court's findings of fact. See Sherlock v. Stillwater Clinic, 260 N.W.2d 169, 172 (Minn. 1977) (deferring to trial court determination of facts to support a negligence decision).

ARGUMENT

I. **THE COURT SHOULD NOT AWARD THE APPELLANTS DAMAGES FOR THE COSTS OF RAISING THEIR NORMAL, HEALTHY SON TO MAJORITY.**

   A. **Frank's Birth Did Not Injure the Appellants Because Giving Birth to a Healthy Child Cannot be an "Injury."**

Because the benefits of a healthy child outweigh any attendant costs or burdens, the costs of raising a healthy child can never be an element of damages in a so-called "wrongful pregnancy" action. The Superior Court correctly joined the vast majority of jurisdictions in adopting a bright line rule prohibiting plaintiffs from recovering the "ordinary costs of raising and educating a normal, healthy child conceived following an allegedly negligent sterilization procedure." Chaffee v. Seslar, 786 N.E.2d 705, 708 (Ind. 2003) (cataloguing the thirty-one states refusing to allow damages for child-rearing expenses associated with raising a healthy child). Many jurisdictions currently limit recovery in wrongful pregnancy cases to child-bearing costs. See Judy S. Loitherstein, Towards Full Recovery—The Future of Damages Awards in Wrongful Pregnancy Cases, 25 Suffolk U. L. Rev. 735 (1991). For three reasons, this Court should follow suit and adopt a rule that precludes awarding the child-raising damages the Bell-Wesleys seek.

First, this Court should affirm the Superior Court's decision that Frank's birth—like the birth of any healthy child—cannot be described as a compensable "harm." Recognizing that "life . . . cannot be an injury in the legal sense," a majority of courts have held that the birth of a healthy child does not damage that child's parents. See Chaffee, 786 N.E.2d at 708 (declining as a matter of policy to award damages for the costs of raising a child). Although raising an unplanned child may be costly, "human life is presumptively invaluable," id., and the "intangible benefits [of raising a child], while impossible to value in dollars and cents are undoubtedly the things that make life worthwhile." See Terrell v. Garcia, 496 S.W.2d 124, 128 (Texas Civ. App. 1973) (holding, in a negligent sterilization case, that the benefits accruing from parenthood outweigh damages accruing from the birth of a healthy child); Rieck v. Medical Protective Co., 219 N.W.2d 242, 244–45 (Wis. 1974) (recognizing that children contribute "to the welfare and well-being of the family and parents" and refusing to allow child-raising costs because that would create "a new category of surrogate parent"). Simply put, "[t]he birth of a healthy child, and the joy and pride in rearing that child, are benefits on which no price tag can be placed." Boone v. Mullendore, 416 So.2d 718, 722 (Ala. 1982) (citation omitted). The result here should be no different: the underlying policy rationale—that human life can never constitute a harm—applies equally to Frank. Although his birth was unplanned, Frank's life is invaluable, both to himself and to his parents. Consistent with this rationale, the Superior Court correctly determined that Frank's birth did not "harm" the Appellants.

Second, this Court should adopt the majority rule because it is impossible for the Appellants to prove—or any fact finder accurately to project—future damages for child-rearing costs. See Hitzemann v. Adam, 518 N.W.2d 102, 107 (Neb. 1994) (refusing to award child-rearing costs in wrongful pregnancy case in part because costs are speculative and difficult to assess). For example, in Girdley v. Coats, 825 S.W.2d 295, 298 (Mo. 1992), the Supreme Court of Missouri rejected a claim for child-raising damages because "[t]he costs of child rearing—and especially education—are necessarily speculative." See also McKernan v. Aasheim, 687 P.2d 850, 853 (Wash. 1984) (declining to recognize damages for raising healthy child because of "the speculative nature of the damages . . . and the possibility of fraudulent claims"). The Appellants contend that general tort principles dictate Dr. O'Toole's accountability for all "reasonable" and "foreseeable" damages; however, the Appellants do not provide any ready means of calculating these supposed damages. This is because no fact finder can foretell the actual costs of raising, educating, feeding, and clothing Frank for the next eighteen years. Although the Appellants offer a government report excerpt that approximates the average cost of raising a child to majority, see R. at 5, this off-the-rack estimate is just that. This report, not specific to Frank, underscores the impossibility of estimating Appellants' claimed damages in this case. Instead, the rule developed in cases like Girdley, McKernan, and Hitzemann, all of which rejected child-rearing damages as too speculative, is the only practical result. Accordingly, the Court should reject the Appellants' efforts to recover speculative damages for raising their son.

Third, this Court should reject the Appellants' attempt to recover for the costs of raising Frank because such damages are disproportionate to the supposed harm of having a healthy child. The Appellants argue that the deterrence goal of tort law demands physician accountability for their full damages. However, where—as here—the recovery they seek is grossly out of proportion with Dr. O'Toole's culpability, the goal of deterrence is ill-served. See Johnson, 540 N.E.2d at 1370 (adopting limited damages rule in wrongful pregnancy suit on public policy grounds); Rieck, 219 N.W.2d at 244–45 (precluding recovery for birth of unwanted child because of excessive burden on physicians, noting that such a recovery "would be wholly out of proportion to the culpability involved, and that the allowance of recovery would place too unreasonable a burden upon physicians").

The costs of raising Frank to adulthood, estimated by the Appellants at over $350,000, R. at 3, are astronomical in comparison to those involved in a vasectomy, a low-cost, out-patient operation performed in the doctor's own office. The Superior Court's award of substantial damages for the pre-natal period, coupled with the injury to Dr. O'Toole's professional reputation, together serve tort law's goal of deterrence. To go beyond the trial court's award and assess liability grossly disproportionate to Dr.

O'Toole's negligence would result in the practice of defensive medicine and increased sterilization costs. Physicians will likely pass these costs on to their patients by charging greater fees for sterilization, denying a socially valuable, low-cost family planning option to patients. Consistent with these considerations, the Court should affirm the Superior Court's decision rejecting the Appellants' claim for damages for raising Frank.

> B. **Even if the Birth of Appellants' Son Constitutes an "Injury," Frank's Birth Did Not Cause A Compensable Economic Injury to the Bell-Wesleys Because They Sought Sterilization for Purely Non-Economic Reasons.**

This Court should affirm the Superior Court's holding that the Appellants should not obtain full child-rearing costs as damages because they sought sterilization for non-economic reasons and were thus not financially damaged. Courts do not award full child-rearing costs where the parents, like the Appellants, sought sterilization for eugenic or therapeutic reasons. See, e.g., Burke v. Rivo, 551 N.E.2d 1, 6 (Mass. 1990) (stating that where the purpose of sterilization was therapeutic, parents should not recover child-rearing costs). Instead, courts award damages for the pre-natal period only. In Hartke v. McKelway, 526 F. Supp. 97, 99 (D.D.C. 1981), aff'd 707 F.2d 1544 (D.C. Cir. 1983), cert. denied 464 U.S. 983 (1983), for example, the plaintiff had suffered an ectopic pregnancy. Fearing that another pregnancy might be fatal, she obtained a tubal litigation. Id. However, her sterilization was unsuccessful and she later gave birth to a healthy child. Id. Because Mrs. Hartke sought her sterilization for therapeutic reasons only, the court limited her damages to the pre-natal period. Hartke, 526 F. Supp. at 105.

Here, the Appellants, like the plaintiff in Hartke, yearned for a healthy child like Frank. Before Frank's birth, the Appellants had tried to start a family three times, only to see each attempt result in the birth of a sick child who died in infancy. R. at 1. The Appellants abandoned their hopes of having a family only when Dr. O'Toole informed them that it was highly probable that any child they conceived would suffer the same fatal congenital illness. Mr. Bell-Wesley, like Ms. Hartke, pursued surgical sterilization solely to avoid the birth of another deformed child, not to avoid the costs associated with raising a child. R. at 11. Thus, the Appellants escaped the injury they sought to avoid. This Court, therefore, should limit their damages accordingly.

II. **THIS COURT SHOULD NOT ADOPT A RULE THAT OFFSETS THE APPELLANTS' DAMAGES BY THE BENEFITS OF A CHILD BECAUSE SUCH BENEFITS CANNOT BE QUANTIFIED.**

This Court should also reject the Appellants' invitation to apply a "benefits rule" that discounts their alleged damages for child rearing by the benefits they enjoy from raising their son, because the benefits received from raising a child can never be weighed against the costs of raising that child. Although a small handful of jurisdictions have adopted such a rule to offset awards of child-rearing damages, see, e.g., Ochs v. Borelli, 445 A.2d 883 (Conn. 1982); Chaffee, 786 N.E.2d at 708 (noting three jurisdictions that apply this rule in negligent sterilization cases), most jurisdictions have rejected this rule because it would "invite speculative and ethically questionable assessments of damages that in the long run would cause a great emotional impact on the child, its siblings, and the parents." Boone, 416 So.2d at 722. Indeed, as noted above, most courts have recognized that human life is invaluable, and thus not subject to monetary quantification. See, e.g., Chaffee, 786 N.E.2d at 706, 708 (holding that "damages for an allegedly negligent sterilization procedure may not include the costs of raising a subsequently conceived normal, healthy child" because "all human life is presumptively invaluable"); Cockrum v. Baumgartner, 447 N.E.2d 385, 388–89 (Ill. 1983); Terrell v. Garcia, 496 S.W.2d 124, 128 (Tex. Ct. App. 1973), cert. denied, 415 U.S. 927 (1974).

Put differently, under the Appellants' proposal, the "harm" to parents alleging wrongful pregnancy and seeking full child-rearing costs is the financial suffering, while the "benefit" is the lifelong relationship with a child. Because this benefit is not quantifiable, the two cannot be compared as a matter of law. See Johnson, 540 N.E.2d 1370. Here, the result is no different. Frank's life is invaluable and should not be subject to monetization. Accordingly, the Court should not award child-rearing damages to the Appellants, even if such damages are offset by the benefits of having a child.

III. EVEN IF THE APPELLANTS' OFFSET RULE APPLIES, THE EMOTIONAL BENEFITS THE BELL-WESLEYS WILL RECEIVE FROM THEIR SON OUTWEIGH THEIR FINANCIAL COSTS.

Even if the Court were to apply the Appellants' proposed damages offset rule, their demonstrated desire for a healthy child requires a holding that the benefits predominate in this case and that damages should not be awarded for the claimed child-rearing costs. In applying this rule, courts look to the reasons for sterilization as well as the benefits enjoyed by the plaintiff due to raising his or her child, and where those benefits outweigh the claimed harms, damages requests necessarily fail. See Sherlock, 260 N.W.2d at 176. In other words, the equitable principle embodied in the proposed offset rule requires that the plaintiff's damages be offset by the value of the child's aid, comfort, and society, which will benefit the parents for the duration of their lives. Id.

Courts regard the reason parents sought sterilization as the most telling evidence of whether, on balance, the child's birth actually damages the couple. See Univ. of Ariz. Health Sciences Ctr. v. Sup. Ct., 667 P.2d 1294, 1300 (Ariz. 1983) (observing that where the reason for sterilization was fear of a genetic defect, the birth of a healthy baby is likely to be a "blessing" rather than a "damage"). Courts also consider the parents' subsequent conduct, such as whether they put the child up for adoption. See Pub. Health Trust v. Brown, 388 So.2d 1084, 1086 (Fla. App. 1980) (noting that the failure to place the child up for adoption indicates that the parents are benefited by keeping the child).

Here, the evidence overwhelmingly suggests that the Appellants benefit tremendously from their son. They have declined to put Frank up for adoption, R. at 8, demonstrating their awareness of Frank's substantial benefits. Moreover, the Appellants sought sterilization for non-economic reasons. When the Appellants conceived each of their three deceased children, they determined that the joys of parenthood exceeded the emotional and financial costs of pregnancy, birth, and child-rearing. Nothing indicates that the Appellants altered this evaluation; they sought sterilization solely because they feared the birth of a fourth sick child. R. at 8. As such, the birth of Frank—a normal, healthy son—has not economically damaged the Appellants. Thus, the Appellants' own evaluation of the costs and benefits of parenthood, evident from their repeated attempts to have a healthy child, demonstrates that Frank's birth was, on balance, a benefit to them. Even should this Court apply the Appellants' proposed damages offset rule, therefore, it should determine as a matter of law that the Frank's benefits outweigh any supposed harm suffered by the Appellants and deny any damages for child-rearing.

CONCLUSION

For the foregoing reasons, the judgments of the Superior Court and the Court of Appeals should be affirmed.

Respectfully submitted,

D. Nathan Neuville

D. Nathan Neuville
Attorney for the Defendant-Appellee